D0448380

Step by Step

Real AAs, Real Recovery

Selected stories
from AA Grapevine

Other books published by
AA Grapevine, Inc.

The Language of the Heart (&eBook)
The Best of Bill (&eBook)
Spiritual Awakenings (&eBook)
Spiritual Awakenings II (&eBook)
I Am Responsible: The Hand of AA
The Home Group: Heartbeat of AA
Emotional Sobriety: The Next Frontier (&eBook)
Emotional Sobriety II: The Next Frontier (&eBook)
In Our Own Words: Stories of Young AAs in Recovery
Beginners' Book
Voices of Long-Term Sobriety
A Rabbit Walks into a Bar
Young & Sober (&eBook)

IN SPANISH
El Lenguaje del Corazón
Lo Mejor de Bill (&eBook)
Lo Mejor de La Viña
El Grupo Base: Corazón de AA

IN FRENCH
Les meilleurs articles de Bill
Le Langage du cœur
Le Groupe d'attache : Le battement du cœur des AA

Step by Step

Real AAs, Real Recovery

Selected stories
from AA Grapevine

AAGRAPEVINE, Inc.
New York, New York
www.aagrapevine.org

IV

Second Printing 2012

AA Preamble

Alcoholics Anonymous is a fellowship of men and women
who share their experience, strength and hope
with each other that they may solve their common problem
and help others to recover from alcoholism.

The only requirement for membership is a desire to stop drinking.
There are no dues or fees for AA membership;
we are self-supporting through our own contributions.
AA is not allied with any sect, denomination, politics, organization
or institution; does not wish to engage in any controversy,
neither endorses nor opposes any causes.

Our primary purpose is to stay sober
and help other alcoholics to achieve sobriety.

Contents

Step One

Step Two

Step Three

Step Four

Step Five

Step Six

Step Seven

Step Eight

Step Nine

Step Ten

Step Eleven

Step Twelve

Welcome

The joy of good living."

This is the theme of AA's Twelfth Step, according to the book *Twelve Steps and Twelve Traditions.* But most AAs would probably agree that this is the theme of all of the Steps.

The Steps have been called inspired by God. "I doubt if the Twelve Steps that have changed the course of existence for so many thousands of lives could have been the mere product of human insight and observation. And they can and will bless anyone, alcoholic or not, who will follow them through and be obedient to them. They are morally and spiritually and psychologically and practically as sound as can be," wrote Dr. Samuel Shoemaker, the Episcopal clergyman who helped in the founding of AA, in the Grapevine in 1964. "I often say and shall always say that the Twelve Steps are one of the very great summaries and organic collections of spiritual truth known to history. ... Herein is spiritual wisdom and health. We have had to look deep within, probe, burrow, struggle, and in a sense this never stops."

Initially, there were six Steps, which co-founder Bill W. expanded into 12 in the process of writing Chapter Five of the Big Book. He originally named God very liberally throughout the Steps, leading to heated discussion and the eventual compromise and the addition of "as we understand Him" and "Higher Power."

"Those expressions, as we so well know today, have proved lifesavers for many an alcoholic," Bill wrote in a 1953 Grapevine article. "They have enabled thousands of us to make a beginning where none could have been made had we left the steps just as I originally wrote them. ... Little did we then guess that our Twelve Steps would soon be widely approved by clergymen of all denominations and even by our latter-day friends, the psychiatrists."

Members sometimes view the Twelve Steps as therapy, perhaps the best therapy available for alcoholics. "Outward problems in our lives are produced by conditions within ourselves. Persistent use of the Steps removes the inward conditions that cause the problems," a 1976 contributor to the Grapevine wrote. "As we experience changes in ourselves, we live our way into a new understanding, and we gradually stop creating difficulties in our lives. We find answers and solutions that we could never see before, and they all come from the program. It's so simple that it's sometimes tough to believe!

"Regardless of where we are in sobriety, you and I have a specific method of dealing with what happens to us each day—by simply renewing our work in the program. Unless I do this kind of continuing work, I'll never know what the AA message really is or how to help another person experience it."

This book shows how AA members of all ages, from all lifestyles and from around the world, followers of mainstream religions and atheists, newcomers and old-timers, have recovered and found a new way of life by working the Twelve Steps. The Steps are a very popular submission topic, with a great deal of manuscripts on Step topics submitted each year. Every issue of the Grapevine since its redesign in 2007 has included a Step story. Here is a variety of experiences that AAs have written about the Steps and sent to the Grapevine over the course of its existence, from the 1940s to the present.

STEP ONE

"We admitted we were powerless over alcohol—that our lives had become unmanageable."

Bill W.'s description of Step One in the "Twelve and Twelve" is rife with metaphors. There's "John Barleycorn," the personification of the grain barley and the alcoholic beverages that are made from it—beer and whiskey. There's the image of the "lash of alcoholism" driving drunks into AA, and the "life preserver" that the dying seize with fervor.

Perhaps the most important metaphor is the image of the "taproot": "The principle that we shall find no enduring strength until we first admit complete defeat is the main taproot from which our whole society has sprung and flowered."

According to an online encyclopedia, a taproot is a large root that grows straight downward and forms a center from which other roots sprout laterally. "Plants with taproots are difficult to transplant ... and uproot."

Admitting defeat is the taproot of the rest of the program, the one Step that AAs must take 100 percent before continuing with the rest of the program. Some AAs realize their lives are unmanageable and that they can't handle alcohol years before entering the program. Others accept the first or the second half of the Step before taking it in its entirety.

"When I first came to AA I was told that I should not bother to try and find out why I became an alcoholic, but rather I should accept my alcoholism as a fact and begin to do something about it," writes the author of a 1966 Grapevine story. An earlier piece in 1944, calls the admission of unmanageability and powerlessness the "first success on the road to well-being."

On the following pages, AAs talk about Step One.

On the First Step

November 1944

The first of the 12 Steps in the creed or philosophy of Alcoholics Anonymous is, "We admitted we were powerless over alcohol—that our lives had become unmanageable." By such an admission any alcoholic, provided he is sincere, has achieved his first success on the road to well-being.

Such an admission is usually very difficult for the alcoholic to make. The very nature of his disease makes him shun the knowledge of his inability to cope with the problems of everyday life. Hence his desire for something that will rapidly create whatever he thinks he lacks as an individual. With a few drinks under his belt he can fashion the most wonderful dreams about himself. These dreams can become his real characteristics—but only when he recognizes that he must dominate alcohol rather than have alcohol dominate him.

The sincerity with which the newcomer takes the First Step is the gauge by which his recovery through AA can be measured.

Over the years the alcoholic develops a three-dimensional ability at picture building, which is a kind way of saying that alcoholics are adept liars. So that by really taking the First Step—admitting freely and without reservation that he is an alcoholic—a person starts to build a new pattern of thought. The whole, at last, is fabricated from truth rather than wishful thinking or fantasy.

John B.
New York, New York

I Had Lost the War!

November 1952

It didn't take me five minutes to admit that I am an alcoholic. It's true that I had always rationalized that I had lost a battle, when in reality I had lost the whole war. Yes, at long last I surrendered unconditionally.

A while ago a speaker said that it was no use admitting that one was an alcoholic unless the admittance was accompanied by a realization of what being an alcoholic really meant. The next time I heard the speaker he persuaded me that I wasn't finished with the First Step yet. He said there was no use my making the admission even in the full realization of what it meant, unless I accepted the fact that I was an alcoholic without resentment. That took a little longer; but finally, after having the resentment removed I thought I could honestly say I had fulfilled the three conditions he laid down. Admission, realization, acceptance. From now on, all I had to do was to take this Step each day, and then devote my thoughts to the other 11. All sweet naiveté! To think that a mind soaked with alcohol would so easily change its habits of thinking and rationalization. John Barleycorn dropped the direct attacks like an experienced campaigner and started a flanking attack coupled with some smooth fifth-column work.

I began to read some other works on alcoholism as well as the Big Book. A natural interest, you might say, for an alcoholic. In all sincerity some of these books as well as seeking a "cure" were also hoping to learn something about "prevention." I began to ask myself—How and when did I become an alcoholic? Did I become an uncontrolled drinker five years ago? Or was it ten? Could I have been born with alcoholic tendencies? These and many more questions surged through my mind.

The same speaker now told me that there was no use in my wondering why or when I became an alcoholic for the very simple reason that it wouldn't change my condition; even if I did find the answer, I would still be an alcoholic.

The clergy, the scientists, the medical profession, the social workers, all have good and legitimate reasons for seeking the answer to "how and when," but do I? The Twelve Steps told me "to try to carry the message." They didn't mention my becoming an expert on alcoholism, its prevention and cure. Actually do I really care about the future generations? Perhaps I should, but truthfully, my charity hasn't developed to that extent yet.

Why then, was I concerned with how or when I became an alcoholic? I know now. Subconsciously or otherwise, I was making a last desperate attempt to get out from under. Somebody else, or something else was going to accept the responsibility for my plight. My fault? Perish the thought. Wasn't it enough that I admitted my condition, realized what it meant, and accepted the fact without resentment? Did I have to accept the blame too?

Apparently I had. Funny thing—it doesn't seem to matter much to me now, "how or when." My interest in future generations is confined to wishing well to those who legitimately seek the answers. I still have too many "selfish" things to look after before I can become "unselfish" enough for that.

Anonymous
Toronto, Ontario

I Was Just Run-of-the-Mill

March 1953

To all outward appearances, many things and circumstances in my life are much the same as they were three years ago: same husband, same house, same economic standard, same community interests. But to me and to my close family and friends who are observing, these things and I are greatly changed. These changes have come about since my faltering and almost disinterested approach to AA.

I did not think myself alcoholic, and if I had, probably would have tried to conceal it, had I not learned that alcoholism is a disease no more to be ashamed of than diabetes or tuberculosis.

My symptoms were similar to those of many others, no very exclusive ones peculiar to my very special case. For some time I was aware of the fact that I could not depend on me especially after that first drink. My former enthusiastic interest in my home, the appreciation of the beautiful rural surroundings in which I live, the enjoyment in my dogs, my music, my interest in the several community projects in which I worked was waning and in some instances had disappeared. Worst of all, my attitude toward my fine husband was changing to the point where my love for him was rather vague and detached. Sometimes I wondered what was happening and became thoroughly miserable over it but I always found that a cocktail or two magically changed the complexion of things, temporarily at least, and it was always tomorrow that I would face reality. Aside from one incident, there was nothing to indicate to the casual observer what was slowly and insidiously eating at my very soul.

Like many others in AA to whom I have talked, it was easy to admit that my life was unmanageable but not that I was powerless over alcohol, the latter for several reasons. I did not drink in great quantities. Sometimes, because it was not convenient, I would not have anything for as long as six months. I had never promised myself nor anyone else that I would not drink again. The only person who had suggested it was my husband and I could see no reason for it. However, after being informed on alcoholism, the first part of the First Step was relatively easy for me.

To receive this education on alcoholism, I spent every day for two weeks from noon until midnight in one of the AA clubs of a neighboring city, where I talked to men and women of all ages and wide experience every night. I went there with the idea of looking over the situation and deciding whether I would be interested in the program or would condescend to associate with any of the adherents. What a revelation to my ears and eyes awaited me!

I was just run-of-the-mill.

Those people were all sober and they were all happier than I had been for at least five years. Toward the end of the two weeks, I had learned that I was an alcoholic, that my case was just run-of-the-mill. I was not special at all. I had also learned that if I continued to drink, it was not impossible, indeed it was highly probable, that my material circumstances would change for the worse, my health would decline and my mind become more befuddled and foggy ... all these if something worse did not get me first! But I also learned that my disease could be arrested, if I would accept the Twelve Steps of Alcoholics Anonymous as a way of life, and best of all I would be happy again, would feel love in my heart, would enjoy God's beauties and would be anxious to give of myself in service to others. I learned I must not only accept the Twelve Steps but must work each one as written, in the order named, each day that it is my privilege to greet; and from that time on, my life should be made up of twenty-four-hour periods.

The simplicity of the whole thing appealed to me. What a relief to "turn everything over" after the highly complicated design I had for living! Now that the days have lengthened into a few years, my husband is beloved and cherished, the house has become a home again and some of the community projects have progressed because of my willing service. Best of all, there have been invisible changes in me and each day my heart sings as I try to do His will for me. All this did not happen overnight. It required diligent working of the Twelve Steps and application of the principles, and the task is far from accomplishment, but the dividends are growing.

Even though I am the granddaughter of a clergyman, the daughter of a clergyman, the niece of four clergymen, and the cousin of three clergymen, God had never been real to me and it certainly had never occurred to me to get him mixed up in my problems. Strange that I should find my God in a group of recovered alcoholics, yet it is the most magnificent and humbling experience I have ever known.

G.R.P.
Richmond, Indiana

Beyond Step One

July 1957

I t has been my contention for some time that AA is not merely a fellowship of ex-drunks gathered together for the purpose of staying sober. It is a program for better living, in which the gaining and maintaining of sobriety is merely the first step—to alcoholics a "must" and all-important one.

The AA program centers on better living rather than sobriety. In the Twelve Steps the words alcohol and alcoholics are each mentioned only once. I think it is logical to assume that they are used in Steps One and Twelve simply because we are a Fellowship of alcoholics and sobriety is our first problem, not our last; nor can they all be solved by sobriety alone.

The other ten Steps do not refer to drinking but dwell on improving our way of living. I will concede that these other ten Steps would help a person stay sober if he saw fit to use them for that purpose and they are no doubt an indirect asset to sobriety; but they are a direct benefit to a better way of life.

The "Definition of AA," as many have seen fit to call it, is for me a complete explanation of AA.

The last sentence in the so-called "Definition" says: "Our primary purpose is to stay sober and help other alcoholics to achieve sobriety." It does not say "Our purpose"—it says "Our primary purpose." In other words, not the whole purpose but the first.

First of what? My answer is—the first of a series of things we must do if we want a better way of life.

R.B.
Addison, New York

Slow Learner

March 1962

S tupidly, my great downfall—after nearly two sober years in AA—came about because of a misconception of the First Step.

In 1945 I had suffered very little from my chronic alcoholism. Sheer luck had saved me from jails, and a loving and patient family spared me from many humiliations which I richly deserved. I had lost several jobs, but each time moved on to better ones.

Early in 1945 when I had just lost a particularly good job with a rosy future because of a month-long binge, I came to AA. In meeting after meeting I heard fellow members tell of gruesome experiences in jails and "booby-hatches"—of wrecked homes, destitution and skid row, and each time they prefaced their remarks by saying, "My name is Joe, and I'm an alcoholic."

Because of staying sober in AA for a while, I prospered in business. And the more I prospered the more I wondered about my experience as compared to my fellow members who kept saying they were "alcoholics" and had been so much worse off than I had been.

At the same time I heard it frequently said that "in the First Step we admitted we were alcoholics." And I began to wonder whether, by comparison, I was really an alcoholic, or had just been using a wrong mental attitude in my drinking. In other words, I was doing a lot of silly rationalizing and dwelling on the comparison of myself and fellow members.

Naturally this led to a "blow-off" in less than two years, and I reverted to drinking, but with increased consumption. My whole object for the ensuing six years was to escape from myself—to bury my shame—as I felt I had failed in AA as I had failed my family, my employers and my Higher Power.

During this six-year interval I lost everything I possessed, not only all worldly possessions, but family, friends and respect in my field of work. I went heavily into debt, well into the five-figure bracket.

Early in 1953 I had reached a low "bottom," and crawled back to AA. This time I read the First Step with definite understanding for the first time. I observed that it said, "We admitted we were powerless over alcohol"—nary a word about being "an alcoholic"! I was not sensitive then—or before—about the word, but before my interest had been in whether I qualified as "an alcoholic" as I heard it referred to in meetings.

Now I suddenly realized that all I had to do was ask myself a simple question: "Am I or am I not powerless over alcohol?" I didn't have to compare myself or my experiences with anyone, just answer a simple question. In 1945 I had had ample evidence in twenty-four years of irrational or "alcoholic" drinking to prove I was "powerless over alcohol." But, I had wasted valuable time wondering whether a certain adjective applied to me.

In 1953, having lived through all of the things I had heard related in closed meetings, and having been beaten right down to the gutter, nothing mattered to me but the hope of sobriety, which I wanted more than anything on earth. In fact, at this point I had to have sobriety to live. A few months before, in a large hospital to which I had been admitted suffering from chronic and acute alcoholism and a liver enlargement more severe than had ever been seen in that hospital, I was given just two weeks to live.

God must have had other plans for me, as I pulled through to come back to AA, free from worry over definitions, and dedicated to helping new members who haven't been hurt too badly. I want them and their families to be spared all of the suffering that will come if they revert to drinking as I did. I will urge them to read the First Step literally, and ask themselves the simple question contained therein—Are you or are you not "powerless over alcohol?"

J.L.S.
Miami, Florida

I Was My Problem

August 1966

There has never been any doubt in my mind that I am an alcoholic since I found out about alcoholism. I think I could best describe myself in the early years by looking at the First Step and just taking the last half of it. I think that from the time I was born my life was unmanageable. I didn't know why and I didn't know that it was. I had a problem from the very beginning and the problem was myself. And that's the reason I think this program works for us, because it helps to remove "I"—I was my problem—and the practice of the AA program helps me to change myself so that I am no longer a difficulty to myself.

When I first came to AA I was told that I should not bother to try and find out why I became an alcoholic, but rather I should accept my alcoholism as a fact and begin to do something about it. I was terrified of what I was going to find in

AA but when I got here I "came home." When I walked into AA I felt that feeling of friendship and fellowship and warmth and all the things that we come to know as part of an AA group. I sort of fell in love with AA right from the very beginning and I have felt that way about it ever since.

E.M.
Wellington, New Zealand

100 Percent

August 1988

I have wanted to take the First Step for almost two years now. In Step meetings some of you said that the First Step was the only one which could be taken 100 percent. I could not take it that fully, though, and I envied those of you who could. I envied you for your DUIs and jail sentences and DTs. You had gone so low you had taken the First Step before your first AA meeting. You weren't fighting alcohol any longer.

For me, however, I thought about drinking a lot. It was still an option.

I used to plan on going to a bar, but one of our chips says, "Call your sponsor before, not after." So I would call, and each time she would suggest not drinking for the next twenty-four hours only. And so it was.

Recently, after my sponsor moved, the struggle with Step One resurfaced. I asked God to help as I could not go on much longer resenting being in AA.

The next day I went to my home group, where one of our members was telling his story for the first time. Toward the end he began to share that he had struggled with the First Step for his first two years, and the point he made was how glad he is now that he never decided to give up during those two years, because the obsession finally did pass. He said that he knew he was an alcoholic when he came into Alcoholics Anonymous, but he didn't quite believe it. And for as long as he didn't believe it, he fought it. Well, in time he not only believed it, but he accepted it. It was then that the obsession passed.

I'm glad he stuck it out because I needed to hear his story. If anyone reading this is still struggling with the First Step, I pray this gives you hope that there will be freedom for you, too.

Carol B.
Atlanta, Georgia

Gateway to Freedom

September 1994

L ying face down on my dirty living room carpet, hands manacled behind my back, I listened as the sheriff's deputies ransacked my home looking for contraband. I heard one deputy remark, "Boy, this dude sure likes to drink. Must be forty empty liquor bottles on the kitchen floor."
Terrorized, my mind raced, trying to remember if there was anything illegal in the apartment. Unfortunately, a week-long drunk prevented any lucid thought at all.

How had I gotten myself into this situation? I had no idea. My world had become a one-bedroom apartment which I protected with half a dozen loaded guns. The hideous Four Horsemen—Terror, Bewilderment, Frustration and Despair—had moved in as nonpaying roommates and refused to leave. I lay in a pool of incomprehensible demoralization, not knowing what to do.

One day a week later, bright and early, the doorbell rang. I looked out through the peephole and saw it was John, a former crime partner I hadn't seen in over six years. He looked very different, was quite fit, and his eyes sparkled. Afraid of what he might want, I conversed with him through the door. He told me that the reason for his visit was to make amends to me.

After further discussion, I finally opened the door. John was stunned at my deterioration. He spent the rest of the day carrying the message to me, telling me the story of his miraculous recovery in the Fellowship of Alcoholics Anonymous. I finally agreed to go to an AA meeting with him that evening, though I couldn't see how it could possibly help me.

At the meeting, I heard the First Step for the very first time: "We admitted we were powerless over alcohol—that our lives had become unmanageable."

The word powerless hit me like a bomb blast. It described my situation with alcohol perfectly and completely. My life was more than unmanageable, it was illegal.

The best part was the word "we." I was no longer alone. Others before me had made the admission of powerlessness and had been set free from years of alcoholic misery. If John could work the AA program and stay sober for six years, then I would have to try my best to do it, too.

Later on I got an older member to help me work the program and formally took the First Step. My sponsor told me that my unmanageable life was a result of self-will run rampant. He went on to say that the only things I had any power over were my behavior and my attitude.

Believing that I was powerless ultimately reduced the size of my world—down to me in the moment. My sponsor explained that alcohol was but a symptom of deeper problems. He also went on to explain that I was selfish, childish, grandiose, emotionally sensitive and had a number of character defects that stood in the way of serenity and peace of mind. But he said I had a choice: to live life reacting to everything with childish emotions, or to try working the remaining eleven Steps and learn how to live a life guided by spiritual principles.

Today I am learning how to develop a better sense of honesty and to accept my alcoholism with all its ramifications. The obsession to drink was lifted almost immediately and the grace of God continues to shine down on me as I learn how to live life on life's terms. The First Step was the gateway into a new sober life that I could never have imagined.

Anonymous
Gainesville, Florida

Who, Me?

April 2000

A t my first AA meeting, the leader asked, "Is anyone here with less than thirty days of sobriety? If so, please raise your hand and give us your first name so we can get to know you better."

I'd had two glasses of sherry before dinner, so I felt I qualified. I raised my hand, gave my first name, and proudly announced, "I am a functional alcoholic."

A year before, I had completed thirty-two successful years of teaching high school. I'd been what society loosely defines as a social drinker since my high school years, and alcohol use had never been an issue in my life.

Instead of retiring, I decided to make a career change and took to travel writing. Soon, I experienced something called "writer's block" and found one way to get through it was with a couple of shots of vodka. It worked, so I imbibed on an increasingly frequent basis.

It wasn't long until I was sneaking bottles into the house and hiding them in filing cabinets. My wife noticed liquor on my breath and that at times I walked funny.

She and I talked, and in order to bring peace to the family, I agreed to go to an AA meeting. The idea of me being an alcoholic was preposterous—alcoholics sleep in gutters, pass out on barroom floors, are homeless, and drive on the wrong side of the road. Me? An alcoholic at sixty? With my record? Ridiculous!

I became more careful about hiding bottles and kept my bottle of mouthwash handy. My wife was as smart as I was, and she soon caught up with me. I agreed that I would go to a rehab facility if I continued to drink.

One day I came home from the store with my spanking new bottle and when the garage door opened, there was an empty vodka bottle standing in the doorway to the house.

That was it—off to rehab.

It was there that my stereotype of an alcoholic changed. I met professional people, bright young folks, others around sixty—a random sample of humanity. Here, it was comfortable for me to admit that I had become an alcoholic—I had acquired the disease.

But I held to the belief that this was like a bad cold—if you blow your nose often enough, it will go away. Also I am different from most people—I know how to handle problems. This thinking, in time, led to a relapse, in spite of working the Steps with my sponsor and attending meetings.

Then came a period of sobriety and another relapse—and another.

One morning I booted up my computer to continue working on an article. I sat there. My brain was like a bowl of mush. Nothing happened. Then I thought of other things that were happening. My golf handicap had risen to thirty-nine. My kids had caught me drinking out of a bottle at Thanksgiving, and I had missed several writers' club meetings.

The dawn came. I had hit bottom.

I found a home group and began to attend regularly and collect chips: thirty days, sixty days, ninety days and finally one year. I fastened these to my key chain, and each time I started my car I reminded myself of my disease. Sobriety feels great and my writing career is in full swing.

I have added a third thing in life that is certain. Death and taxes are two. The third thing that is certain is that if you are an alcoholic, you are an alcoholic.

D.D.
Vacaville, California

Surrender to Life

September 2007 (PO Box 1980)

In January 2005, I was asked to leave a rehab before completing the twenty-eight days. My counselor said I was disruptive and unwilling to get honest.

Alone, cold and angry, I reluctantly headed for a meeting at a nearby psych center, thinking maybe there would be coffee and donuts. I was late, and everyone stared at me. I began to walk out in fear, but someone yelled, "Get back in here!" He was a scruffy-looking, long-bearded biker type. As everyone looked on, he asked, "Are you an alcoholic?"

Terrified, I answered, "Yes."

"Then sit down!"

At the end of the meeting. I raised my hand and said, "My name is ChrisAnthony. I'm an alcoholic, I'm hungry, I have nowhere to go, I'm scared, and I really want to drink. But if I do, I'll die."

Within seconds, the whole group surrounded me, hugging me, giving me phone numbers, and offering me jobs and places to live. Only an hour before I was homeless. The more they offered to help, the harder I cried.

Within two months, I had my own apartment, and my sponsor, Patrick (the same scruffy-looking biker), hired me as his electrician's helper and gave me a station wagon. That meeting became my home group, and I did electrical work for the members.

Patrick passed away a few years ago, but not before I did my Fourth Step with him. My First Step was done at that first meeting, when he asked, "Are you an alcoholic?" and I answered, "Yes."

ChrisAnthony S.
Bronx, New York

STEP TWO

"Came to believe that a Power greater than ourselves could restore us to sanity."

Few indeed are the practicing alcoholics who have any idea how irrational they are, or seeing their irrationality, can bear to face it," says the essay on Step Two in the "Twelve and Twelve." "Yet no alcoholic, soberly analyzing his destructive behavior, whether the destruction fell on the dining-room furniture or on his own moral fiber, can claim 'soundness of mind' for himself."

"I was a little surprised that my dictionary defined (sanity) as the quality of being sound of mind, sound of judgment, reasonable and rational in one's thoughts," an AA wrote in a 1982 Grapevine story. "As I sat there mulling over the definition, an idea occurred to me: 'This is what I'm to be restored to—sound, reasonable, rational thinking.'"

AAs writing about Step Two in the pages of Grapevine have often mentioned similar revelations—of how insane they were while drinking and of being restored to sanity through the working of the remaining Steps of the program.

Still others focus on the first part of the Step—about coming to grips with the idea of "a Power greater than ourselves."

It is not a requirement of membership that we believe anything, the "Twelve and Twelve" assures us. "All you really need is a truly open mind." And members can make AA itself their Higher Power, the book goes on to suggest.

Any AA—believer, atheist or agnostic—can take this Step, as the following stories reveal. "The hoop you have to jump through is a lot wider than you think."

On the Second Step

December 1944

Having taken the First Step of the AA program by admitting that we were powerless over alcohol, we were confronted with Step Two: "Came to believe that a Power greater than ourselves could restore us to sanity."

This Second Step is often referred to as the first spiritual Step; but is it or the subsequent Steps any more spiritual than Step One? Is not anything spiritual which tends toward elevating us to the best and highest type of human being we are capable of becoming?

The Second Step contains the crux of the AA method of getting well: it shows us how to expel that little streak of insanity which caused so many relapses into debauchery long after the normal drinker would have shrunk from another drink. This twisted kind of thinking is eliminated by faith in a Power greater than ourselves.

The question which naturally arises in the newcomer's mind is: "How can I acquire enough faith to get well?" The road to faith is by taking all Twelve Steps. Faith is acquired by working for it; it is retained by continuous use of the Twelve Steps.

One who has gained faith in this greater Power finds such faith reflected toward himself. To the alcoholic this means faith that he will not take the first, fatal drink. But that is not all, for soon we learn that in some mysterious way our whole lives have been changed, our thinking changed, and our desires as well. Finally the realization comes that we no longer drink—because we just don't want to.

The greater Power now becomes for us the court of final appeal. Those harsh judgments of people, conditions and so on, which we made in the past, are now left to this court. This is the way to tolerance. Our own ideals, aims and ambitions are also submitted. This leads to progress, and it is by progressing that we become—and remain—well.

Horace C.

I Nearly Quit

September 1965

Came to believe that a Power greater than ourselves could restore us to sanity."

When I first encountered this Step, I took offense at the word sanity. If the Step had said, "Power greater than ourselves could put us back on our feet," or "back on the right path," I could have understood. Sanity, with all that the word implies, seemed too strong.

I felt I couldn't be crazy or I wouldn't have sought help. Truthfully, I very nearly quit the program, all over the word insanity.

It was not until the Fourth Step (after stumbling and skipping over the Third) that I began to see the light. But it wasn't until the autopsy had gotten well underway and I found out that though I appeared normal to see and talk to, I was extremely selfish, thoughtless, heartless, inconsiderate and resentful of the very air I breathed. Was this the moral make-up of a normal person? I decided not. I had lost all true perspective in daily living. I couldn't plan and carry out one full day without confusing my hours with a lot of unrelated side issues and off-the-track thinking. Yes, I finally agreed that I needed the restoration of my sanity.

Then fear set in. Cold, unreasoning fear. What to do? Where to begin? Suddenly I became angry. Angry with myself. Angry with AA. "I might have known," I thought. "I get myself involved with some offbeat outfit and here I am, more confused and upset than ever." I recall wondering, "What's wrong with these people anyway? Why can't they handle their own affairs and let me handle my life as I see fit?" At that point I marched back to Step Two.

Another snag! I knew that somehow if I were to have any semblance of success with the program, I had to believe in a Power greater than myself. I didn't kid myself there. I knew that the answer to that was God and God alone. How to contact Him? I didn't know. I knew about prayer and the universally accepted benefits to be derived from it. I also remembered such phrases as "in God's own time" and "all things cometh to him who waits"—but I wanted my request for restoration of sanity to be stamped "To God for immediate action." With that thought in mind, I really believe I sat back and waited for the flash of lightning and the peal of thunder heralding a spiritual awakening.

Up to this time, my prayers had consisted of half-hearted attempts for relief from my hangovers, from financial strain due to drinking and from marital difficulties brought on by my folly. However, I began to pray in earnest. At first, haltingly, ill-worded and selfishly, but ever so earnestly and sincerely, I laid bare my sins and misspent life. I gave vent to my fears and frustrations, my trials and tribulations, praying that if there ever was a stupid fool who needed help, I was that fool.

Still, I could see or feel no change in myself or my attitudes. I kept coming to AA. Each time I went to a meeting, I insisted to myself that this would be the last time. Later, as each "last one" went by, I finally found myself looking forward to the next "last meeting." And so I have come to accept the Second Step, and to see that through staying in AA, sanity has been restored. I think I'm a better man for the struggle to understand.

J.S.

Walla Walla, Washington

Sanity

March 1981

Around the tables, Step Two cannot be emphasized too much, not only to newcomers, but to all AAs. Clearly, the chief mark of restoration to sanity is our not taking the first drink. No matter what else happens to us, as long as we refrain from the first drink, our lives will get better.

I realize the problems and solutions in my present life may well appear to be madcap, but I know a Power greater than myself is aiding me to carve out a better life. The change from the absolute madness in those tormented years of active alcoholism has been gradual, rather than sudden. When an inventory is taken, I perceive definite transformations—but in reality, they have been slowly coming all along.

I try now to explain frankly that I have problems with my thinking. (And I suspect most AAs have and will continue to have such problems.) But there is a difference: Today, I recognize the unreasonableness of much of my thinking or, more accurately, my responses to others. For me, there is a direct coupling of the Tenth Step and Step Two. The more sanity, the quicker the admission that I am wrong. It is much easier today to get rid of overreaction at the thought level before it becomes a spoken word and then a physical act.

Now, I can see that sanity is steadily being restored to me so that I can use the other Steps to greater advantage.

Sanity Clause

February 1982

The "sanity clause" in my "contract" with AA simply tells me that if I want to maintain my sobriety, I must go to any length to keep my mental attitude constantly aimed toward sound, rational thinking in all my affairs, one day at a time.

If anyone had told me thirty years ago that AA would come to mean basically that to me, I would have thrown up my hands and said, "What an order! I can't go through with it." As it has turned out, however, from the day—November 16, 1950—when I first came into contact with AA, it has been my privilege to be an active member. For this, I am truly grateful.

The word sanity had very little meaning to me during my early years in AA. When the occasion arose to discuss Step Two, we would talk about the word insanity, but little time was spent on sanity. Someone usually set the theme by telling about his or her insane escapades, and then each of us in turn would follow by recalling our own insane acts. Sometimes, it would take on the appearance of a contest, the object being to see who could out-insane the other members.

Then, one night after a Step Two meeting, I decided to find out what those courageous early members who put our Twelve Steps together really meant by sanity. I was a little surprised to find that my dictionary defined it as the quality of being sound of mind, sound of judgment, reasonable and rational in one's thoughts. I was further surprised to find that the definition of sanity did not even mention insanity. As I sat there mulling over the definition, an idea occurred to me: "This is what I'm to be restored to—sound, reasonable, rational thinking."

Since that time, I have used my dictionary to check on the meaning of other words in our Twelve Steps, our Traditions, and the first part of the fifth chapter of the Big Book. I find that this gives clearer meaning to my program as a whole. This habit of checking the meanings of words has caught on with other members. One of our women members even donated a fine dictionary to our group, to be used along with our Big Book and other AA material.

W.H.
Shenandoah, Iowa

An Indescribable Benevolence

August 1992

C ame to believe that a Power greater than ourselves could restore us to sanity." What does this Step mean to me, a woman with just nine months of sobriety in AA behind her? What was my process of "coming to believe," and in what way do I feel I am being "restored"?

At first I had to take this Step on faith alone. I knew I believed; but I did not begin to understand. Why would God bother with someone who had misused her energies, squandered opportunities, bruised the hearts of loved ones and ridden alcohol like a runaway horse to the gates of insanity and the brink of death?

Slowly I began to realize that "why" was the wrong question. One day when I was about three months sober, a quiet gentleman spoke up at my noon meeting and delivered a message which seemed to have my name written all over it. He said that we need only ask ourselves "how"—and that this question could be answered by three simple words: "honesty, open-mindedness, and willingness."

I was desperate enough to try anything—even follow directions. I began to share at meetings as honestly as I was able. The pain and ugliness that poured forth from those dark recesses within appalled me, but to my amazement, no one judged. My worst confessions were received with tenderness and even a certain reassuring humor. I began to see that all of us had suffered in many different ways, and that I was hardly unique in experiencing that terrible sense of being "in disgrace."

But wasn't "dis-grace" the opposite of God's grace, God's blessing, God's love? As I strove to keep an open mind, or at least to prevent the door from completely slamming shut, more things were revealed to me. My own active role in forsaking God became all too apparent. It seemed that I had "disgraced" myself, not so much through the recklessly hurtful actions I committed in my drunkenness, but in closing myself off from the infinite, mysterious how of divine love.

In opening my mind to new ways of loving and being (and sometimes, in my willingness, I could only manage the merest crack), I felt the gentle infusion of an indescribable benevolence. It was as if, in spite of myself, unconditional love insisted on streaming in through that crack in the door and filling the aching void, the God-shaped space in my heart. I felt his love in the embraces of fellow AA members, I witnessed his grace in the serenity shining from their eyes, and in the rollicking laughter which sometimes threatens to lift the roof at my home group meetings; I heard the music of recovery.

Willingness was simply given to me. I began to feel that my feet were keeping me sober; they unfailingly took me to a meeting even when the rest of me screamed in protest. As this willingness was planted in me and slowly, haltingly grew, I began to feel the subtle dawning of an amazing inner light: a sense that I was being restored.

How could God do this? Had I ever really been sane—and if I hadn't, where was the model for this restoration? Surely he had nothing to go on, no plan to follow. I began to doubt again, to wonder whether I even had enough inherent worthiness to warrant this miraculous process.

Then I began to realize, through other people's loving messages, that no one is entirely self-made. A woman in my Step group expressed it this way: "Who we are is God's gift to us. Who we become is our gift to God." It began to dawn on me that recovery is something like the restoration of a very old painting, covered over by layers and layers of darkening, distorted varnish. This process of restoration is so precious in God's eyes and is undertaken with such infinite care that not all of the underlying pattern can be revealed at one time. What is uncovered, bit by bit and layer by slow, careful layer, are the things which are necessary and appropriate for me to know about myself right now.

Moreover, no painting paints itself; we are masterworks, all lovingly created by God's hands. Whether our colors are vivid or subtle, whether the design is boldly abstract or serenely pastoral is not our choice. Ours is only to accept this work of art as given—to strive to reveal our true colors and the beauty of our true design in everything we say and think and do.

I do not begin to understand the miracle of this restoration in my own life. I only know that it is happening, and that it is not a mistake. A sense of my own worthiness is restored only very slowly; it is as if God knows I must be responsible for past damage and be more careful in the future if I am able to feel truly worthy. Though God loves me unconditionally, I will have to live my own faith, cherish each day of my recovery, and practice unconditional love to the best of my limited ability before I can wholeheartedly love myself.

The process is slow and often painful, and sometimes I feel I have barely begun. But when frustration or impatience overtake me, or when ego threatens to override all the progress I have made, I try to remember that God is the master painter—the spirit which inspired the works of Michelangelo, Renoir and Van Gogh—the loving force which is even at this moment restoring the damaged painting of my life to its original luster and irreplaceable design.

Who better to carry out this loving and painstaking restoration than the master himself?

Margaret G.
Port Coquitlam, British Columbia

Beyond Sanity

February 1999

T here are those, too, who suffer from grave emotional and mental disorders, but many of them do recover if they have the capacity to be honest." That quote from the Big Book describes me. I have a mental disorder—severe clinical and chronic depression—but I am in recovery. The program works. When I first came into the Fellowship, I was in a depressive state, and a few days later was hospitalized for the fifth time. In the hospital, I learned about the illness of alcoholism: the mental obsession and the physical compulsion. When I was re-leased from the hospital a month later, I began attending AA meetings in earnest.

At first, staying sober was not as difficult as I had envisioned. The physical compulsion had left me while I was in the hospital, and though I was left with an occasional thought or desire for a drink, there was nothing upon which I had to act. Within a short time, I began to notice some benefits of sobriety that were special to me and became self-reinforcing. Without ingesting alcohol, which was a depressant, my depression finally had a chance to improve. It wasn't over yet, but through the grace of God, I could see change. More than that, sobriety seemed to coincide with freedom from the hospital. I had stopped attempting suicide (something I'd only done while drinking). And now, thirty-seven months into sobriety, I haven't been back in the hospital.

Taking the First Step was easy. Hospitalizations and drunk driving citations had clearly made my life unmanageable, and I knew I was powerless: that the first drink would get me drunk.

It was the Second Step that I eyed with intense interest: "Came to believe that a Power greater than ourselves could restore us to sanity." Did that mean that my Higher Power would eradicate my mental illness? That is what I believed and prayed for. If the God of my understanding could offer me recovery from alcohol-ism, could he not offer me recovery from this other illness as well?

As I continued to attend AA meetings and listen carefully, I heard experiences with the Second Step that didn't quite apply to me. One common definition of in-sanity was "doing the same thing (i.e., drinking) over and over, expecting different results." That definition fit me as far as my alcoholism went, but was too narrow to help with my mental illness. I resigned myself to a continuing mental illness.

However, I also continued my journey with the Steps. Doing each to the best of my ability, with painstaking care, I completed all twelve, until in the end

I found a new definition of sanity. It was bigger than any definition I had heard concerning Step Two, but it was also bigger and better than my wildest imaginings. This sanity offered serenity, a feeling of wellness or well-being, possession of a center of balance from which to operate, and a feeling that my place in this world was just right. The sanity I've received through work on the Steps is far more than I could have hoped for.

Now I'm not only a recovering alcoholic but have truly been "restored to sanity," and am forever grateful.

Doreen C.
Bowie, Maryland

Two Ounces a Day
July 1993

After a little sobriety, some of the craziness of the drinking days gets to be funny. It feels good to laugh about it, but it's bittersweet humor with an edge of pathos and lunacy not far below the surface. When someone bristles at the word "insanity" in Step Two, I remember that I did, too—and I think of this episode.

A few months before I stopped drinking I took my first physical in years. I took a bunch of tests, and my liver put some bad numbers on the board.

Did I drink? the doctor asked.

"Some," I said.

He said he wanted me to limit myself to two ounces a day, or risk serious damage to my liver. "Would that be a problem?"

"No problem," I said.

I didn't want to blow out my liver, but I didn't want to give up martinis, either. So I tiptoed up to the edge of the limit the doctor had set: Each day I took my bottle of gin and my measuring cup and poured precisely two ounces for my single, skimpy martini. I felt deprived, of course, but kept it up for a week.

Then I got to thinking. The doctor said two ounces of alcohol, and this gin was only eighty proof—just forty percent alcohol—so I was shortchanging myself. I did the math. To get two ounces of real alcohol, I'd have to drink five ounces of gin!

So I measured out that more generous serving for another week or so, but still felt cramped. I was a busy guy, after all, and didn't have time to fool with measuring cups. What the doctor really meant, I decided, was to limit myself to two drinks a day. So I forgot about the measuring cup and made myself two martinis a day—in a glass the size of a goldfish bowl.

Of course, even that discipline soon was abandoned.

My mental gyrations made perfect sense at the time, but a little sobriety made me see the bizarre episode for what it was: A doctor told me I faced serious health problems because I was drinking too much, and I responded by playing games.

If he had told me that chocolate bars were causing a life-threatening problem, I wouldn't merely have cut back; I would have quit, that day, because chocolate bars weren't that important to me. And that's the insanity: Alcohol had become important enough to me to die for.

G.S.
Royal Oak, Michigan

Where's the Miracle?

November 2006 (PO Box 1980)

In AA, I often hear, "Don't give up five minutes before the miracle." But most of the important and astounding things that have happened to me in the last eighteen years of sobriety in AA have been slow in coming and impossible to recognize or appreciate until long after they took place.

However, there was one exception. That is the miracle that comes with Step Two.

One day, after nine months of attending meetings and staying dry, I was standing alone in our meeting room just beneath where the Twelve Steps hung on the wall. I looked up and my eyes fell on Step Two.

As I read, "Came to believe that a Power greater than ourselves could restore us to sanity," I suddenly realized that I no longer had any desire to drink. I couldn't even remember when I had last thought of alcohol. The obsession which had controlled my whole life for twenty-five years had simply vanished. AA works.

Dennis D.
Fort Worth, Texas

STEP THREE

"Made a decision to turn our will and our lives over to the care of God as we understood Him."

S tep Three calls for affirmative action," the essay in *Twelve Steps and Twelve Traditions* states. "It is only by action that we can cut away the self-will which has always blocked the entry of God—or, if you like, a Higher Power—into our lives."

The Big Book uses even stronger words about self-will: "We alcoholics must be rid of this selfishness. We must or it kills us!"

And so, AAs move toward the action Steps, where they prepare to take inventory, admit the nature of their wrongs, ask for help in removing their character defects, and make amends.

The AAs in this chapter talk about the various parts of Step Three: making a decision, what it means to turn over their will and lives, and God as we understand him—or, for many AAs, as we don't understand him.

"I was too confused to be even a good agnostic," an AA wrote in a 1981 Grapevine story. "The turning of my will and life 'over to the care of God as we understood Him' implied that some sort of understanding had to come first." It was only after years of searching that she let go of her need to understand God. "Everything is easier now that I have a Higher Power that I don't understand."

"Good" replaces "God" in some AAs' beliefs. Other use AA itself, or "Ultimate Purpose of the Universe," or "Collective Wisdom" as their Higher Power.

"I notice that there are a lot of people who ... spend their time trying to find this 'God they understand' in order to turn their will over to him/her," an atheist AA wrote in a 1998 Grapevine story. "There doesn't have to be a recipient of their will: All they have to do is let it go."

In these stories, find out how other AAs have approached Step Three.

The Anecdote Bin

August 1964

Bill R., Norwalk, Connecticut, says he heard another fellowshipper say, "My group is so advanced, we begin with the Third Step."

Breaking Through Ritual

December 1966

For over a year in AA I fulfilled the Third Step by submitting my life and my will to the care of God, as I understood Him.

It was a fighting year! Fears were still my most frequent companions. Doubts battered my thoughtful moments. Turmoil boiled inside the cheerful exterior.

Prayers were an uncomfortable ritual with me. I feared not to pray and was rebellious when I did. With clenched teeth I was saying to the strict God I feared, "OK! It's your show anyway! You're going to make it end up your way—so—here I am. Show me what you want me to do and I'll try my damnedest to do it. If I can't do what you ask of me, well, just remember I'm only human!" That was my "surrender" prayer most of the time.

But there were fleeting moments of faith and a desire to love. "Oh, God, teach me to love you. Enable me to place my life, my heart, my mind and my will, into your care. Help me to know You as You really are; not as my fears and doubts paint you. Lord, I believe; Help Thou my unbelief!"

During that first year plus, I learned some self-control and self-discipline; something I'd never learned before. Many of my character defects grew smaller. I lost fifty pounds and learned to laugh again. I believe I became a more interested and mature mother to my six children; a companion and understanding wife to my AA husband.

I got an outside job for the first time in eleven years. I grew emotionally and mentally. And unknown to me, I was maturing spiritually! At thirty-three I was tasting life in all its reality for the first time and I was staying sober—me, whose last drunk had lasted a year and a half; who had been hospitalized for drug addiction after six weeks in AA. It was a miracle!

Life was not all roast beef and gravy, but it was digestible. My spiritual awakening was breaking through. Maybe God had a heart after all! Maybe He did care about insignificant me!

But the doubts lashed over my mind and soul again and again, making me cringe and tremble, fight and rebel intermittently. Finally, at one AA discussion meeting I dropped the smiling facade and called them all a bunch of Pollyannas. I wasn't happy or peaceful inside and was sick of using self-hypnosis. I didn't want to drink but I finally had to admit out loud that happiness was a farce. They were all just playing the part at the AA "Humble-Hour."

I'd always gone to seven or eight meetings a week, and during the next few weeks I let them all have it. I ventilated all the spiritual doubts and turmoil; the fears and resentments at God. I got honest in my own unusual way! And a strange thing happened.

Many of the older members knew exactly what I was going through and told me what was happening to me. They told me it was an important step in my spiritual growth for I was beginning to think for myself. I was becoming acquainted with God as I understood Him—not as my parents, pastor, brother, neighbor, husband or friends understood Him. Suddenly, I was questioning all of my childhood beliefs and faiths. Did I really believe these things for myself?

The house built on sand was crumbling and God was laying the foundation of my home on a rock.

A few weeks later during my evening meditations, which were usually uncomfortable, I abandoned the old pattern of ritual and instead, on my knees, poured out my heart to God. I wanted to trust Him to take care of my children, my husband and myself for now and eternity. I knew there'd never be peace or freedom for me without that faith.

Sometime during that long night I knew I'd been stubbornly submitting my life and will to God. I'd learned well the rules of my new life over the previous year, but I'd been a fearful student, terribly frightened of the Master!

Yet, strangely, I'd totally surrendered my alcoholic problem to a "different" God. The God who took my drinking problem was a loving, merciful and understanding God, for He'd given me freedom from the compulsion to drink.

Needless to say, I didn't believe in several Gods. For me there was only one God! So it had to be me who was out of focus.

What, I asked myself, was the real difference between submit and surrender? In *Webster's New World Dictionary* I found: to submit is to give in to authority or superior force (to submit to a conqueror); and, surrender commonly implies the giving up of something completely after striving to keep it.

After more than a year of submitting to a superior force, I let go of the old fears and rebellion and voluntarily surrendered myself, body, mind and soul, to a loving God.

There is one tremendous difference for me between submit and surrender: When I submitted to God I was still festering inside with ideas of how I wanted my life to be and the events that should take place. I was still first. But I was a prisoner of me.

Yes, there's still a superior force in my life, but now it is a gentle, sympathetic and loving God. He doesn't crack a whip or demand anything of me. I gratefully and lovingly give all that I am and have to Him. I've learned that if I give these gifts to Him grudgingly, then they're of no value. Only a gift given in love and gratitude is blessed to the giver and precious to the receiver.

At last, I'm acquainted with freedom and peace.

F.B.
Orchard Lake, Michigan

The Leap into Strange Waters

October 1972

I've heard the Third Step referred to as the "Here come the tambourines" Step. To me, the first time I met it did seem to recall days of the missions and saintly soup. But my jaundiced eye is seeing more brightly, and my mind has improved with the added light. Still, this great commitment to letting some power outside of me take over my life and will is a jump into strange waters.

How wise the founders were to put this Step in third place. But even after the First and Second Steps, I found the words of the Third Step too hard on ears that had stopped hearing or "understanding" and too soft on a heart that had stopped hoping.

Then came a revelation—Step meetings. To me, this was the teaching of the skill needed to use the tools that the Third and all of the other Steps have become. On my own, they were like a calibrator given to a child with no instructions on the box.

The Third Step became more than the word "God." It became my first decision, or at least my first try at making one.

I listened to many. I tried this way and that, but no one else's understanding seemed to fit into my own newfound honesty efforts.

I looked at the words, trying "hope" instead of "understood," "group" instead of "God," "surrender" instead of "decision." And, while none of these quite fit, I suddenly realized that all this work had taken time. Although the fit was not right, the trying was, and the life and will I now had to turn over were different.

So different, in fact, that one day someone said to me that something I had done was a good thing. What it was or who said it, I don't recall, but the word "good" was understood as turning a familiar corner, a landmark when I thought I was lost. "Good" was "God" with only another "o." I could be good-like. I had tools, I had the ability to be honest, to feel in my guts what was good or bad. I had a measure or scale inside of me, something so simple I could follow it without reason or plan.

Some time has passed, and my understanding of God has not much improved, but my understanding of myself has. I know now the measure of good in men is God. With enough sober time, enough effort at honesty, the Third Step is taking me.

C.W.O'D.
Ardmore, Pennsylvania

Humor

June 1978

Overheard from an Al-Anon member: "When I took the Third Step, it took the management of my life, for the first time, out of the hands of an idiot."

D.C.

Ham on Wry

October 1986

Did I really hear that?
D. O. of Alberta says she heard the following at a topic meeting on the Third Step. The speaker announced that he'd turned his will and his wife over to the care of God.

Keep Coming Back

April 1991

I was pretty sick and confused in my early sobriety, and so to keep everything really simple when it came to the question of God, I paraphrased the Third Step this way: Whoever it is up there who took care of me as I staggered from barroom to barroom, who guided me while I drove home in a blacked-out condition, who stopped me from seriously injuring my wife and children, who kept me from killing myself when I was dangerously out of control, please continue with this daily care, because now I'm aware of the intercession and I'm truly grateful for it.

Today, my even shorter version of the Third Step is this: Keep taking care of me, Lord, because I appreciate it now.

Gary M.
Berrien Springs, Michigan

Sharing Hope

February 1993

Each morning I follow the suggestions on page 86 in the Big Book; then I usually take a two-mile walk along a beautiful nature trail. There's a special huge oak tree where I pause and say the Third Step prayer in the Big Book:

"God. I offer myself to Thee—to build with me and do with me as Thou wilt. Relieve me of the bondage of self, that I may better do Thy will. Take away my difficulties, that victory over them may bear witness to those I would help of Thy Power, Thy Love, and Thy Way of life. May I do Thy will always!"

I am very comfortable going to six noontime meetings each week in my little hometown. I cannot say one is better than the other; they are all great meetings: A Twelve Step study group, two Big Book meetings, and three speaker-discussion meetings. I came into AA when I was fifty years old and I haven't had a drink or even a desire to have a drink for twenty-one years.

Recently, I had to fly from San Francisco to Miami for a six-day job in a convention center. Well, my Higher Power had other more important plans for me.

About three days into my job I had a mild stroke. The whole left side of my body, leg, and arm went limp and numb.

This happened to be a physicians' convention and I was immediately surrounded by many doctors. An ambulance appeared as if by magic and the next thing I knew I was on the sixth floor of a hospital. I was in a two-bed room and the other bed was empty. The nurse told me that all the patients on that floor were elderly heart patients. Because I had mentioned in the ER that I thought I had heart problems, they put me there with a heart monitor hanging around my neck and an IV towering over my head, dispensing some sort of liquid in my veins. I looked and felt sick.

Now I started feeling sorry for myself. "Poor me, I'll never be able to work again, and besides they'll probably put some old geezer in here with me (I'm only seventy-one years of age) and I won't get any sleep because of his snoring and groaning and so on."

As I was wallowing in self-pity, they rolled in a man about thirty years old, dirty, unshaven, and very, very loud. He was talking all the time. So I closed the curtain between our beds. I was one sick cookie and I didn't want to hear anyone else's problems.

Then the miracles started happening.

My telephone started ringing. Word had reached my home group in California that I was in a Miami hospital and one call after another came in, sending the kind of love and caring that we share in AA.

One man called and said, "Hi, this is George from California." I didn't recognize his voice so I had to ask him, "Which George?" My family called and said my phone was constantly busy. More AA calls came in and more love was exchanged. I realize now that regular attendance at meetings leaves a permanent effect on more people than is realized—God takes care of that.

The man in the bed next to me started getting curious as my emotions burst out into the open. The curtain parted slowly and our eyes met. His phone had not rung once. He said, "You sure have a lot of friends" and his eyes welled up. He told me that his father and mother had not talked to him for years and he had no friends out there at all who trusted him.

I told him that besides my family calling, all these calls were from Alcoholics Anonymous and that I had been a member for a number of years. He told me that he had been hospitalized from a drug overdose. Prior to coming in, he had been comatose for three days before someone found him and rushed him to the hospital—to the bed next to me.

Whenever my phone rang, he said he listened to every word that was said and could not believe the love and emotions he heard. Then the second miracle happened. He told me he wanted what I was getting from across the country. He said he was addicted to drugs and wanted to do something about it. (Alcohol was not mentioned then.) He asked about the Twelve Steps, and I said, "Oh, you've heard about our program?" "Yes," he said, "I spent ninety days in jail and the AAs came in there."

As time passed, he asked how AA got started. I told him how Bill W. and Dr. Bob met and carried the message of sobriety to the third man in a hospital bed. It was during that conversation that I got very emotional, looking into his eyes and thinking of the actual story of AA number three. Like AA number three, my friend was afraid to leave the hospital. He said, "My record is so bad that I'm scared to leave. I know I can't go it alone out there."

My experience gained in meetings and knowledge of the Big Book were called upon. One time he looked at me and I could feel the pain in his sad and worried look. I said, "You're worried again," and he repeated what I must have said to him many times: "I know—a day at a time it will get better." I told him that sometimes we have to do it a minute at a time.

I must have mentioned chapter three about the denial of our disease and its progression, because at one point I told him he had run out of gas! He started laughing and repeating it. "Where did you hear that term?" he asked. "They say that in jail!" He laughed some more and shared with me some of his experiences in jail. The next thing I knew he was calling me "Houseman," a name the inmates call the convict that's been there the longest. One time I asked him for a sweet roll that he left on his tray, and he said. "Anything you want, Houseman!"

A nurse came by, heard the laughter in the room, and said, "It's a miracle that you two are here together."

"The Twelve Steps are worrying me," he said. I tried to quiet him by saying what I had heard after asking the same question at four months' sobriety: "You have taken the First Step. You're not here to worry, you're here to get well."

Another day passed and he admitted he was also an alcoholic. Then he told me his whole life story and how he had lost everything. When he finished, he said, "I have never in my life disclosed these things to anyone before—they just came out."

He looked worried again and I said, "Now what's the matter?" Tears filled his eyes and he said, "I wish my father would talk to me like you do."

"It takes time," I said.

I was to be discharged the next day and he didn't want me to leave. I said I'd call another AA member to come by and see him. I began calling the central office, the Alano Club, and even halfway houses, trying to get hold of anyone who would drop by. It was a long holiday weekend and I couldn't reach anyone.

Then another miracle happened. A counselor from somewhere showed up with a Big Book. I immediately took the book and opened it up to chapter three for him to read but in its place was an upside-down page from one of the stories in the back of the book. I think that was God's way of saying that he wasn't ready for this right now, thank you.

Morning came and I was to be discharged. A social worker appeared and said she had one opening in a ninety-day county program and my friend could go directly into it, right from the hospital the next day. That was another miracle, but there's more. Just before I left, his sister visited and placed a phone call to his dad and his dad actually talked to him.

We hugged goodbye and exchanged addresses and phone numbers and he smiled and I could see that he would be all right. I knew then that he was safe and in God's hands. My Third Step prayer was answered.

About my mini-stroke. The numbness only lasted five hours. Tests proved that my heart is perfectly normal and strong. The reason I was kept there for six days was for extensive tests and ... well, you read my story!

Hal R.

Millbrae, California

Free Thinking Allowed

March 1998

O ver fifteen years ago, I "took the Third Step" with a sponsor, without asking much about her belief system. As time went by, I realized I'd been subjected to some of the principles and practices of her Higher Power, not mine. (I was still searching, so perhaps I was considered fair game.) This happened several more times, and I've come to believe that people in recovery need to ask prospective sponsors about their belief systems to help them assess whether that sponsor will work for them. At least they'll have the choice to decide whether the issue is relevant to them or not. My son has become a second-generation member of AA, and watching him go through similar experiences with sponsors trying to push their own religions has brought me out of the silence at last.

This is not meant to be divisive. AA is one of the few places where freedom of spiritual practice has at the least been given lip service, in keeping with the ideals of a free society. If members need to be reminded that the ethics supporting such freedom suggest not foisting religious beliefs on others, then those concerned about it need to speak up.

I've seen entire meetings decide they were Christian or decide to shun someone with different beliefs. I don't know if this is in the spirit of group autonomy, but I finally told my son that if he doesn't feel like taking on an entire meeting, he can move on to another one that welcomes more diversity or even start his own. Meetings for "freethinkers" have even appeared from time to time—thankfully, making recovery possible for people not too sure what that "higher power" business is all about. After all, even within a homogeneous community—like an all-Christian meeting, for instance—"higher powers" can differ radically.

J.W.
San Francisco, California

An Atheist Lets Go

June 1998

Years ago, when I first began to play with the idea that I might be an alcoholic, I spoke with a few people who were members of AA hoping to gain an insight into my problem. But with each person I spoke to I ran into a roadblock in the form of the Second and Third Steps. The usual message I received was that it was all right to be an atheist as long as I believed in God. Neat trick.

I tried to point out the contradiction in this idea but I was told that I couldn't work the AA program without some sort of higher power, whether I called that higher power God or something else.

"Why not use a chair as your higher power," they'd tell me. (For some reason they always used a chair as an example.)

I had two problems with this suggestion. First, it was an insult to my intelligence. Second, I wondered just what kind of concept of God they had if they relegated God to the status of a Lazy-Boy lounger.

At the time, I was seeing a counselor who was trying to get me into AA. She thought there was an atheist group somewhere in town but she wasn't sure where. I decided that if there was a higher power he didn't want me to join AA. If he did, he would have created a group that denied his existence!

I was hospitalized for about seven weeks for depression. Though my alcoholism wasn't treated, I was able to give it some serious thought while I was there. I left the hospital accepting the fact that I was an alcoholic but not knowing what to do about it. I rejoined a therapy group I'd belonged to and the very insightful counselor who facilitated that group had dug up information on a special interest AA group for atheists and agnostics. He knew that my only rational defense against joining AA was my atheism, so when he gave me this meeting information I decided I was going to check it out.

I won't go into detail about how nervous I was at that first meeting or how everyone welcomed me and made me feel comfortable, not only with my alcoholism but with my atheism as well. Knowing they'd been through the same thing made me stay.

My first four months in AA were exclusively at this meeting. I couldn't imagine attending traditional meetings. But as time went on I began to feel more secure in my feelings and was encouraged to attend "God meetings" occasionally. My first such meeting was at the local Alano Club, and it was on the Fourth Step.

"Good," I thought, "I won't have to deal with the Second and Third Steps." And I didn't. Obviously, by admitting I was an alcoholic, I had completed my First Step, so now all I had to do was just concentrate on the Fourth Step. (Actually I was going to concentrate on how to avoid the Fourth Step—but that's another story.) But the concept behind the Third Step was still a problem for me.

I'd always been a willful and manipulative person. I pulled my first con job at the age of three. I developed this little song and dance that not only made my family adore me but also allowed me to turn them against my older brother. But I was now beginning to see that my days as a star were over. I had no job, no money and no home. I was living in a shelter, picking up cigarette butts out of the gutter, believing that I had no future at all.

Since I didn't have a higher power to turn my will over to, I decided to just let my will go in any direction. It didn't matter where it ended up, I just wanted to get rid of it. Maybe I could make other people take responsibility for my actions, so I started doing everything people told me to do. I followed every suggestion in an almost zombie-like fashion. And there was never a shortage of advice.

"Don't drink," I was told. No sweat. I didn't have money for booze anyway.

"Go to meetings," they'd say. No problem. It was better than hanging around the Salvation Army center with all the crazies.

"Listen to what is said at meetings." I had no choice. I was a zombie.

At first the things I heard went in one ear and out the other. But then something amazing happened. They began staying in my head. Good grief!—the things I was hearing began making sense. Things about honesty, integrity, and fellowship. Promises about serenity, intuition and security.

Security? I was getting a little worried about my security. I mentioned to my first sponsor that the shelter would be closing in a week and I had no place to go.

He said, "Mention it at a meeting. Someone might respond." Good advice. I mentioned it at a meeting and someone not only offered me a place to stay for a while but a temporary job to boot, helping him work on his house. It turned out to be ideal. He lived only two blocks away from the Alano Club so I was able to go to as many meetings as I wanted.

Since the job was temporary, I knew I'd have to look for another one. Once again I employed my sponsor's suggestion. It was at one of the special interest meetings that I casually mentioned that I'd soon be looking for a job as a legal secretary. A woman handed me a business card. Two days later I had a good job with a prestigious law firm.

The same thing happened with my apartment. Someone suggested I check the bulletin board. I found a business card on the board for an apartment building. I was only planning to stay there until the end of summer until I could find a decent place to live but I ended up liking it so much I'm staying for a year.

Then there was my involvement with the atheists and agnostics group. I got the service bug, you might say. When I realized that the Alano Club didn't have a meeting for atheists and agnostics, someone said I should start one, which I did. A friend said I should become the new meeting's GSR. I took his suggestion and became the GSR. I got so enthusiastic about this new position that a week later I even asked my friend what a GSR was. He told me but I realized that it was too late to back out.

I notice that there are a lot of people who approach the Third Step from what I think is the wrong perspective. They spend their time trying to find this "God they understand" in order to turn their will over to him/her, not realizing that there doesn't have to be a recipient of their will: all they have to do is let it go. And that's what I did, I let it go.

Here's Step Three as it might be read for those who believe as I do:

"Made a decision to entrust our wills and our lives to the care of the collective wisdom and resources of those who have searched before us."

That "collective wisdom" taught me so much. But the most important thing is this: when we give up our will we don't give up our responsibility. And though I'm starting to gain more control over my own life, I still listen to, trust and follow the advice I get from that collective wisdom.

But I'm past my initial year of sobriety, and I know I have to accept the responsibility of becoming part of that collective wisdom. And I have to be ready for someone else to drop his will into my lap, someone who's going to trust me. I know that as long as I don't forget the advice I was given, I can't possibly give bad advice to someone else.

So I'd like to end by giving some advice to all of you. Take a break, have some coffee and just turn it over.

Gene J.
Chicago, Illinois

STEP FOUR

"Made a searching and fearless moral inventory of ourselves."

P eople talk about having a spiritual experience after taking the Fourth Step," an AA wrote in a 1997 Grapevine story. "What happened to me was that I learned about the person I had been." When she looked at her assets, she realized that she hadn't set out to harm others or intentionally behaved in an unacceptable manner. She came to see that she wasn't a bad person.

"I was a sick person trying to get better. I was a worthwhile human being."

Step Four, she wrote, gave her a better sense of direction about the areas of her life she needed to work on.

The Big Book describes the Fourth Step as "an effort to discover the truth about the stock-in-trade ... to disclose damaged or unsalable goods, to get rid of them promptly and without regret."

Whether they use the columns laid out in the Big Book—starting with a list of resentments—or use the "seven deadly sins" as a guide to illuminating flaws of behavior, AAs who have gone through the process agree that taking the Fourth Step, though painful, provides a humble look at themselves, a black-and-white list of where they can improve in the future.

In addition, it is an exercise in forgiving the harm that others caused us, and looking only at ourselves. "Where were we to blame? The inventory was ours, not the other man's."

Members have different approaches to Step Four and writing an inventory. Some of these experiences, and the emotional growth that followed, are discussed in the upcoming pages.

Southern AA

August 1950

S tep Four is the hardest for many of us to take after we come to the realization that we are alcoholics. After years of dishonesty with ourselves it is mighty difficult to bring all our faults and shortcomings out into the open and face them fairly and squarely. Yet when we finally accomplish this, we find it easier to face our fellowman and live the AA program in its entirety.

M.D.A.
West Palm Beach, Florida

It Takes What It Takes

June 1978

I could both laugh and cry over my first approach to the Fourth Step: "Made a searching and fearless moral inventory of ourselves." Being a writer and accustomed to an elaborate style, and having a do-it-myself complex, I decided I was supposed to write about my dramatic and unique life. I didn't ask questions or attend Step meetings. I just settled in and supplied myself with plenty of paper and the typewriter. Some 180 pages later, rough drafts strewn all around me, I surfaced to see where I had been.

Sobriety does interesting things to the mind—clears it up some, lets a bit of honesty and truth filter in, and begins to demand reality. What I had written was a dramatic story of someone else, of the person I had taken to the clergyman, the psychiatrist, the doctor for help for my "troubles." Being totally dishonest about myself, I found no relief. It was only when I really wanted sobriety, admitted I was an alcoholic, and realized my unmanageable life was completely beyond me, that doors began to open.

My fiction pages portrayed the person I had conned myself into believing I was, the poor martyred soul who found no rest in a troubled world. At first, I was shocked and horrified at what I had written. Then I recognized that this tormented character demanding center stage was at last out on paper and could be dealt with. Maybe, if I followed directions, I wouldn't have to live with that person any longer.

With the glaring example before me of what happens when I shoot off on my own do-it-myself road, I began a Fourth Step inventory that made more sense. With pencil, paper, and a prayer that I would write down only what actually happened and how I felt about it, right along with dates, places, and boring details, I labored on. I followed examples in the Big Book. And this time, I did not attempt an inventory without the support and help of sober members of AA and the sharing at Step meetings that abound in my AA neighborhood.

I began to get down to the alcoholic that I am, the childish person who reacted poorly to life. A beautiful release happened as I approached myself with a newfound humility. At last, I had found some willingness to peel off the trappings of self-deceit and rationalizations. I discovered some truths about myself. I tended to blame people, places and things for my unhappiness. I thought it had been necessary to drink to alleviate my misery. In the beginning, people in AA let me go right on believing that, knowing that I would trip over these old ideas when I took the Fourth Step again. And indeed I did.

I began to see how AA members, formerly sad like me, were happy, joyful and capable, having serenity enough to live with unresolved problems. They had done their homework, this Step in particular. "You grow or go," they told me. And I received courage from the promise that "we will not regret the past nor wish to shut the door on it." Painful as my journey was, I knew at last the healing power of following the path set before me.

But I had no idea how to accept responsibility for myself, so the knowledge that no one else could dictate how I felt was both relief and burden. Then someone said, "Misery is optional." I cringed, recalling all the misery I had heaped upon my own head. Yet, as I carried the Fourth Step into the next directed action, the Fifth, I heard myself talk about how I allowed myself to wallow in self-pity and despair. I began to gain by pain, to win by losing, to get control by letting go of control. And good feelings poured in from all sides. I discovered how many words that I had been fond of using were actually traps, setting off negative thinking—"If only ...," "You always ...," "never," "forever," "If you would only ...," and so on. I dug in and tried desperately to change word habits, to share time instead of spending it.

Today, I am relieved that I don't have to carry around that dramatic and so often drunk person. I believe in the restorative power of the Steps and can now take a continuing inventory so that fifty years don't pile up on me as they once did. I live and breathe in an adult world, instead of cringing in the corner of an emotional playpen. What a blessed relief to find I am not that dramatic actress after all!

Today, I am a sober alcoholic who desires to stay that way, and I often reflect on the healing experience of the Fourth Step. Now, I believe that "it takes what it takes," and for me, the grueling ordeal of writing a "novel" to get the phony me out of the way was worth every word and agony. It wasn't a very good novel, either; the main character was too emotionally immature to be very interesting.

B.P.

Pompano Beach, Florida

Taking Stock

November 1979 (PO Box 1980)

I n the July 1979 Grapevine, a letter on the Fourth Step said, "I have never read in the Big Book or the 'Twelve and Twelve' that we must write down our assets." I had heard this many times before, and I have, over the years, given it thought. When I walked into AA three years ago, I was angry, frightened, foul-mouthed, bitter and suicidal, a broken woman at twenty. My self-worth was between low and nonexistent, but I did have my moments—where I was the chosen one, the knower of all, the most intelligent, most forgiving, most beautiful, etc. The program has taught me to appreciate balance in my life. I am not the worst and not the best—but where do I fall between those two points?

An honest answer, to me, is the purpose of the Fourth Step. We cannot just keep chipping away at defects of character without developing something to replace them. Assets are the only item I can find to develop, and the Fourth Step seems to be the ideal way of monitoring where I am at with both assets and defects.

I showed that article to my sponsor, and her response was: "I think it does refer to assets in the Big Book, when they talk about a business taking an inventory. In this inventory, they don't just look at the broken and damaged items; they also take stock of what they do have." This, to me, says they get rid of damaged and unusable items (defects) and take stock of the good merchandise (assets), so they know what to get rid of, what to keep, and what to get more of.

J.C.

Lincoln, Nebraska

Burn that Trash!

June 1984 (PO Box 1980)

A Slug from the Jug of Patience" from the February Grapevine included an item about saving Fourth Step inventories. I was once of that persuasion, but there came a day when, at the behest of the man I took as a sponsor, I burned the pages. He felt that saving inventories was tantamount to saving trash, and destroying them came under the heading of clearing away the wreckage of the past.

I was so moved by the burning that I later burned my early inventories. They had served their purpose, and the Tenth Step is what I now use to check out changes in thinking from day to day. This is a one-day-at-a-time program, not one year at a time.

R.O.
Yakima, Washington

Mirror, Mirror, On the Wall

October 1987

Sometimes taking somebody else's inventory can be most beneficial. When I was doing my Fourth Step, an old-timer suggested I list the names of those against whom I held resentments, followed by two or three sentences describing what they had done to earn my displeasure. Then, after putting the list aside for a day, I was to cross off each person's name and replace it with my own.

As I reread the list as if it had been written about me, I began to see things differently. It was the start of an attitude whereby I'm not so quick to judge others. If I'm critical of you, it's often because I'm trying to ignore that quality in myself.

J.R.
Renton, Washington

Naming the Negatives

April 1997

The Fourth Step attracted me almost as I arrived at the doors of Alcoholics Anonymous. I came to AA full of guilt and remorse for all the bad things I'd done—for example, being an unfaithful wife, not doing my job to the best of my ability and still expecting the highest rewards, and being unresponsive to other people's needs. I was totally self-centered, while at the same time I was thought of by others as being a good wife to a man who drank too much and ran around, being loyal to a job for twelve years, and being so sweet (I never expressed an opinion!). But the way I was viewed by others was not the way I felt inside.

I heard AAs talking about getting rid of the guilt of the past by taking the Fourth and Fifth Steps. I wanted to get rid of my feelings of fear, frustration and depression, and I became willing to go to any length to accomplish that.

The first thing to do was to make a decision that since I couldn't handle my own life (look at the mess it was in), I could find my own higher power to which I could turn over my life and my will. After that, I'd be able to look at myself and take responsibility for my past actions.

I certainly didn't know how to put names to my feelings because for years I'd practiced not giving information to others about how I felt and what I thought. If I had problems, I was to solve them myself; hadn't I been taught to be self-sufficient? As I went to meetings and heard others talk about their feelings, I came to recognize some of mine. I came to understand that my natural instincts "for the sex relation, for material and emotional security, and for companionship" need not run my life in a negative way.

Early on, one of my ways of staying sober had been to write down my feelings and questions and new things I learned. At the beginning of my sobriety I would ride home from a meeting on a bus. My small notebook in my purse was there to write down any thoughts I'd had during the meeting I'd just left.

After about fifteen months (and a couple of journals), I went to someone with a good solid sobriety and asked for help in turning my notes into a Fourth Step. He suggested that we meet and I arrived, notebooks in hand. He started me talking, leading me in a discussion of my problems in the areas of sex, society, and security (as suggested by the Big Book). He suggested that I look at pride, greed, lust, anger, gluttony, envy, and sloth. We talked for about three hours and covered every area of my life I had problems in. I found I could put names to my negative feelings and see their source.

What a relief to tell someone about myself without any threat of retaliation or condemnation. I realized I wasn't the worst, most immoral woman alive. I was no different from others who shared at meetings, neither worse nor better, and I wasn't strange or different. When I looked at my assets, I realized that I hadn't set out to harm others or intentionally behaved in an unacceptable manner. I wasn't a bad person; I was a sick person trying to get better. I was a worthwhile human being.

People talk about having a spiritual experience after taking the Fourth Step. What happened to me was that I learned about the person I had been. I looked at my "emotional deformities" so I could "move toward their correction." I now had a better sense of direction concerning what areas I needed to work on. As *Twelve Steps and Twelve Traditions* explains, "… a brand-new kind of confidence is born, and the sense of relief at finally facing ourselves is indescribable."

Since that first inventory, I've taken many Fourth Steps. When my marriage was in trouble, I looked at my part in the problem, at where I'd been wrong. I had no fear in looking at my behavior because I'd been trying in sobriety to be a good wife and companion. I found that my dependence on someone I considered stronger was misdirected. I was frightened of life and hadn't grown up; I felt dominated but in some areas I myself was the one who dominated. I put demands on another person which couldn't possibly be met. I tried to manipulate my husband to meet what I thought were my needs, when I really didn't know my needs.

A few years later, when my marriage had broken up and I'd met someone in whom I was interested, I took an inventory of my relationships with the other men who'd been in my life (father, brothers, friends, lovers), whether they caused trouble or not. I didn't want to get into a relationship where I made the same mistakes over again. In this inventory, I found the same dependencies growing out of fear, self-pity, worry, greed, possessiveness, anger and a lack of confidence in myself.

Today, when a particular problem can't be covered by a daily Tenth Step, I find it natural to use the Fourth Step. I start with the First Step and see where I'm powerless, I recognize that a Higher Power can help me, and I use the Third Step prayer as a preliminary move toward the Fourth Step. After taking a Fifth Step, I use the subsequent Steps to help me handle the problem.

The Fourth Step lets me look at myself, look into my fear of not getting something I want or of losing something I have, get a perspective on my character defects, and move forward to try to establish true partnerships with other human beings: all in order to be "one in a family, to be a friend among friends, to be a worker among workers, to be a useful member of society."

Sherry G.
Riverdale, Michigan

The Other Man's Inventory

April 2007

Don't take other people's inventory!" chides an AA sponsor to an AA sponsee, sometimes gently, sometimes fiercely. As champions at figuring out the faults of others, we alcoholics in recovery often have to be reminded to look at our side of the equation. "The inventory was ours, not the other man's," says the Big Book on page 67. On the other hand, it is a time-honored axiom that we often see the faults in others that we ourselves have, so perhaps when we take someone else's inventory, we are really taking our own. I decided to test out this proposition, with remarkably good results.

As an experiment, I decided to deliberately take the inventory of a fellow member of AA, then put my name on it. I wrote down exactly what bothered me about that person: he wore his religion on his sleeve, he thought he had practically invented AA, he talked endlessly about politics, even in meetings. My anger toward this person was exacerbated by the fact that his politics and religion were virtually the opposite of mine. I typed up a neat list of his defects of character on my computer. Then, I erased his name from the top of the list and typed in my own. I printed the list and carried it in my schedule book for two weeks, reading it daily. Each day, I saw my name above a list of his defects. The first few days, I told myself these were really his defects, not mine. But after four or five days of reading the list, some insights into my own behavior appeared. I saw that I also talked too much about religion and politics around the meetings and sometimes even in the course of my sharing at meetings. I had offended lots of people doing that, but I had always blamed them, saying to myself that they just didn't like me. I had not looked at how my own behavior might be the cause of their rebuffs and scorn. I saw that I also tended to pontificate at meetings, as if I were a very knowing old-timer who really knew how to work the program. By the end of the two-week period, I knew whose defects I had listed: my own.

More important than even the insight into my own character that this exercise provided was the change in my relationship with that fellow AA member. Before starting the experiment, I could not be in the same room with him without feeling a great deal of rage. I often avoided his presence for that reason. However, I was involved in a new meeting that he had started, so it was actually necessary for me to interact with him on certain days of the week. During the course of the experiment, I suddenly lost my anger. I felt absolutely no emotion whatsoever toward this individual. I accepted him precisely as he was, neither approving nor disapproving. I was too busy concentrating on the list of defects, which I was beginning to own as mine. By the end of the two weeks, he had changed toward me as well, congratulating me on a fine sharing here, asking for my advice on something there, and generally being an all-around good fellow. It was truly miraculous.

Since that experiment was successful, I have tried the technique twice more when I found myself extremely angry with someone. It has worked just as well as the first time. In each case, I discovered some unpleasant truths about myself, was able to accept the other person without judgment, and made changes in my own behavior and attitudes that have greatly improved my growth in the life of the spirit.

John B.
San José, California

Heard at Meetings

March 2008

I was so sick when I was new, at one point I asked another guy in my home group if I could copy his Fourth Step.

Michael K.
Haverhill, Massachusetts

Number One Offender

October 2008 (PO Box 1980)

Every time I've done a Fourth Step inventory and looked at my part, I seem to be facing the same three fears: fear of not being good enough, fear of abandonment, and fear of dying. For me, underneath resentment is fear and I believe fear is the number one offender; it lurks in all of my character defects.

The Big Book says, "We asked ourselves why we had (fears). Wasn't it because self-reliance failed us?" Every time I do an inventory, I face this question again. Self-reliance is not listed as a character defect but it seems to be my biggest one. Why be afraid of God? Because of my three basic fears: I believe I'm not good enough, I don't deserve God's love, and God may abandon me when I need him most. If I surrender fully to God then I (my ego) will die.

Trusting God, playing the role he assigns, asking him to remove my fear—these are actions I must take every day. Have I commenced to outgrow fear? In the essay on Step Six in the "Twelve and Twelve" it says that I must try my best, "to make progress in the building of character," plus, I'll "have to be content with patient improvement." So I pray that God reveals how my fear may be useful to others.

R.C.
Kalamazoo, Michigan

At Wit's End

November 2009

After completing the Fourth Step, Johnny was faced with some big chunks of truth about himself. Hoping to hang on to a few of his character defects, he visited his doctor seeking validation.

"Doctor," he cried. "I'm just not able to do all the things around the house that I used to do."

When the doctor's examination was complete, Johnny said, "Now, Doc, I can take it. Tell me in plain English what's wrong with me."

"Well, in plain English," the doctor replied, "you're just lazy."

"Okay," said Johnny. "Now give me the medical term so I can tell my wife."

Christopher K.
Lexington, Kentucky

Her Own Part

April 2010

It was years before I could do an honest Fourth Step. But I guess since I kept trying to get it right, that counted as a desire to be honest. My sponsor would say to me, "This is the same stuff you brought in last year—when are you going to let this go?" The problem wasn't letting it go; the problem was that I couldn't be honest about it. I kept trying to be honest and to find my part in my failed relationships, but I was compelled to blame others and to stay the victim. This went on for years, and it was painful. I had an ego that wanted to be right all the time, and I was miserable.

The main resentment I had was toward my ex-husband. I believed I had wasted my youth on a drunk who had battered me physically and emotionally throughout our marriage. I tortured myself with this resentment for the first 10 years of my sobriety. I was exhausted and ashamed for not having let it go like I heard other people do in meetings.

For a while I blamed my parents for not empowering me, but I knew they'd done the best they could. I had to stop blaming others. When the pain of holding onto the resentment got greater than the fear of looking at my part in it, I had to get rigorously honest and put the blame where it belonged—on myself—for allowing the abuse to go on and for not leaving my husband the first time he laid a hand on me. My resentment wasn't about my ex. It was about how I betrayed and abandoned myself by staying in the abuse and by numbing out on alcohol. I was told in AA that once I owned my part, I could forgive myself because I had been impotent to protect myself at the time.

I kept hearing it was an "inside job," so I got busy learning how to take care of myself, empower myself, and protect and love myself. The women in AA were my teachers, and some wonderful books on codependency helped.

Every morning I go to the mirror, look myself straight in the eyes and say, "I love you, and I promise I'll never abandon you." With this empowerment and without the weight of resentments, I am truly happy, joyous and free. God willing, I am finally able to be of service to others.

Beth P.
Santa Barbara, California

STEP FIVE

"Admitted to God, to ourselves, and to another human being the exact nature of our wrongs."

W
e pocket our pride and go to it, illuminating every twist of character, every dark cranny of the past," says the Big Book, as members who have just written their Fourth Step inventories now proceed to share their histories with someone else they can trust. This sharing, vs. simply admitting your faults to God, is vital to the recovery process. "If we skip this vital Step, we may not overcome drinking."

Nearly all of us have felt in the past that we didn't quite belong, points out the chapter about Step Five in the "Twelve and Twelve." Step Five was the beginning of true kinship with man and God. It was how we "began to get the feeling that we could be forgiven, no matter what we had thought or done. ... Scarcely any Step is more necessary to longtime sobriety and peace of mind than this one."

"Progress in AA is, to me, as if my life had been unfired clay. A crisis comes, and, where once the brittle clay of my life seemed to shatter, I have now come to believe that a Power greater than myself can help me shape my life—and I have decided to let Him do so," writes an AA in a 1979 Grapevine story. "In Step Four, we inventory all the material, and in Five, we begin the process of selecting what we want to keep and what must go. In Six, Seven, Eight or Nine we start eliminating the useless and using the useful. In Ten, Eleven, and Twelve, under the guidance of a Higher Power, we begin a lifelong, daily job of building a new life."

"The feeling that the drink problem has disappeared will often come strongly," adds the Big Book. "We can look the world in the eye."

The Fifth Step—A Way to Stay High

June 1974

Our co-founder Bill W. indicates in the Big Book that a return to drinking is a definite possibility if the Fifth Step is not taken conscientiously. I believe this. I have had faith in the AA program since my first meeting. In the depth of my despair while drinking, and not thinking that I was an alcoholic, I was sure there was a force somewhere that could help me. It never occurred to me to stop drinking. The sheer logic of that never entered my mind. And I did not consider AA. But I was searching. When I arrived at AA, I knew the mirage of help had become a reality.

I realized that I needed all of AA if I wanted more than bits and pieces of sobriety. That meant taking all Twelve Steps. I began reading about them. I am sad for the people who do not read the book *Twelve Steps and Twelve Traditions.* This is the most meaningful book I own. It is a million wise books in one. It's miraculous how AA books grow in impact every time I read them.

I was interested in Bill's explanation of the Fifth Step in the Big Book. In meetings, I told people about my drinking exploits, but something at the perimeter of my mind kept nudging me and saying, "They know all this. This isn't the Fifth Step. Tell them … something painful!"

I took the question to my sponsor. He talked about the misguided drive that some people have to tell all, over and over and over again. He advised me to look for "the exact nature" of my wrongs, instead of just drawing lurid pictures. In preparation for the Fifth Step, he said I should think through the Fourth, counting my assets as well as my liabilities ("something painful"). "The Steps are there to help you, kid," he said, "not hurt you."

I had already gone the clergy, doctor and analyst routes. Now I wanted that "other human being" to be an AA. So I finally picked one and began talking as honestly as I could. When I finished, guess what this guy said. (I don't have to tell any long-time member.) He said, "Is that all? Wait till I tell you about me …."

I felt as if I had discovered the secret of man being able to fly without a machine. What a high! And a safe one. I had been introverted and tense. I had been blocked by a fat ego that made sharing impossible, by a lack of communication, by a fear of love. The Fifth Step swept away all those barricades.

With some humility, I could begin to find joy in the simple delights of life. Sober-and-serene is much better than drunk-and-depressed. I plan not to drink today. The safest way I know to avoid it is to keep my ego down while building up my self-esteem, and the surest way to do that is to continue taking the Tenth Step—a comforting continuation of the work I finally did in the Fifth Step.

I believe in God. I have no secrets, and I fear no man. I am not anxious about death. I am alive, forever, within this 24 hours. And I stay high all the time, high on life, thanks to the Twelve Steps of Alcoholics Anonymous.

E. S.
Brooklyn, New York

Finding Self-Forgiveness

October 1977

"When it comes to ego deflation, few Steps are harder to take than Five. But scarcely any Step is more necessary to longtime sobriety and peace of mind than this one."

–Twelve Steps and Twelve Traditions

My last three years of drinking were a vicious cycle of falling flat on my face, picking myself up, picking up the nearest drink, and then falling right back down. A piece of me was lost in every drunken escapade, and it was not long before every semblance of human resilience, spirit, and dignity had been drained from my life.

Even though I was only twenty-one at the time, my alcoholism had done its job quite thoroughly, and when AA was offered as a possible solution, I grabbed at it blindly, praying that it might have an answer for me. It did.

But then, as the months swept by, I came to the painful realization that my confused and misdirected personality was not going to let me forgive myself for some of the things I had been involved in during my drinking days. These things would not be relegated to the caverns of the past; they could not be laid to rest. So, in order to keep this shame and guilt from spilling out into AA and the group, I built another wall around myself. Oh, it didn't look all that bad from the outside. Meetings were actively attended; newcomers were helped; my responsibilities to the group and AA were attended to; and thanks only to the grace of God, three years of dryness were accumulated.

By this time, however, I had learned that AA is not a program based solely upon external affairs, and it was clearly obvious that I was going to have to crack this wall wide open if I was going to hold on to my sobriety much longer. The hurt, fear and anxiety had grown to such proportions once again that I became "willing to go to any length" once again—even so far as to take the Fourth and Fifth Steps in the manner that, I had been taught, they are supposed to be taken.

This time, nothing could be held back. This time, I would be "fearless and thorough." For the sake of my sobriety and everything else I had come to hold dear and precious, it had to be!

The crack in the wall came during and after the taking of my Fifth Step with a local priest. This experience gave me the release and clearheadedness to see that if the wall was to come down all the way, I was going to have to go further and share the entirety of my past experience and my grosser handicaps with a close friend in AA.

Before actually going through with this plan, I half expected to come out of the experience with an even greater sense of apprehension, guilt and regret. But if I was to be satisfied that I had done what I had to do, and if my mind was to be calmed, I knew I had to put this extra measure of trust in a fellow AA. From past experience, I knew that God would give me the strength to handle the results.

The actual experience of turning myself inside out for the first time in the presence of an AA member left me drained and numb; but when feeling started to come back, I found that I had changed. For the first time in my AA experience, I could feel the sunshine of God's love on my wounds and true peace of mind.

The day ended as quietly as it had begun. I laid my head down on the pillow that night confident that I had just surmounted a major hurdle in my continuing recovery. I was now one step closer to understanding the majesty of God and the miracle of Alcoholics Anonymous.

D.S.
Memphis, Tennessee

List Our Assets?

July 1979 (PO Box 1980)

Whenever I attend an AA meeting where the Fourth or Fifth Step is being discussed, someone always mentions writing down our assets along with our defects.

My life before sobriety and the AA program was spent pampering myself. As soon as I would entertain thoughts about my wrongs, I would quickly dismiss them by remembering all my good deeds. What a cop-out!

Let's face it, these are uncomfortable Steps. Fears of being "too hard on ourselves" only complicate matters. I heard and read that the Fourth and Fifth Steps were necessary for my continued sobriety. This fact made the pain bearable. I have never read in the Big Book or the "Twelve and Twelve" that we must write down our assets when doing our moral inventory.

Being painfully honest in the Fourth and Fifth Steps started me on the road to humility. I could finally accept myself as human and go to work on my varied defects of character (Step Six).

P.H.
Waukesha, Wisconsin

Short Takes
July 1980

When I took the Fifth Step with all the thoroughness I could muster, that part of me I feared the most no longer frightened me. I suddenly realized that God loves me just as I am.

R.P.

A 5,000-Mile Discussion
December 1982

How true it is that we really feel ourselves grow spiritually after honestly carrying out Step Five. My sponsor always said that unless we have done this Step, we can never fully realize how far on the broad highway to serenity we have gone. He also said that most of us find it comparatively easy to admit to God and to ourselves the exact nature of our wrongs, but if that is all we do, we might gloss over some touchy and purplish chapters in our lives.

There is a normal inhibition: We cannot brace ourselves to discuss every detail with a person we know well. I have solved this by choosing a mature and wise sponsor with whom I had been in correspondence. I admired his letters for their perspicacity and perspicuity, and I could really bare my soul to him in writing. By the mere process of writing at length on the wrongs I had committed, including those that had sunk into my subconscious, I found an exhilarating catharsis—a purification of my mental conflicts.

I did this in slow phases, and he counseled me from 5,000 miles away, giving me the benefit of his wisdom and his long experience in AA matters. How eagerly I looked forward to his letters, and how earnestly I took his advice—which I still follow now—to end each day with a brief period of silent meditation. I review my actions of the day and thank God for the wisdom of his will in guiding my actions. I try to be sincerely contrite for any wrong action caused by rashness on my part, be it with anger, procrastination, pride, envy, or the many other shortcomings that my human flesh is heir to.

I cannot adequately describe how light I feel since I took the Fifth Step, and how soundly I sleep. It has almost helped me share the gift of levitation that the birds of the air are blessed with.

It took time and effort, but the Big Book tells us we must constantly strive for progress, through the Twelve Steps. When I finally molded this delightful habit, my sobriety was permeated with a growing sense of well-being, in which I have experienced more than mere glimpses of serenity. I have shared this thought with my AA friends, and they tell me that they, too, have found great peace of mind through really having carried out the Fifth Step.

I am intensely grateful to AA and my Higher Power and my sponsor for having guided me in this difficult Step. The modus operandi was devised to suit my own personality; but I would urge readers to give the Fifth Step a genuine try. The Higher Power, as you understand him, will surely guide you to another human being whom you can trust and rely on to guide and counsel you without raising his eyebrows over the purple patches.

K. G.
Secunderabad, India

Ham on Wry

November 2000

Nervous about hearing his first Fifth Step, a young priest asked an older priest to sit in on the session. After the AA member had described a few of his experiences, the older priest motioned the young one to step out into the hall.

"Cross your arms over your chest and rub your chin with one hand like this," the older priest directed him. The young priest tried it. "Good," said the older priest. "Try saying 'I see. Yes, go on.' And, 'I understand. How did you feel about that?'" The young priest complied. "Now don't you think that's a little better than slapping your knee and saying, 'No way! What happened next?'"

Shirlene H.
Bountiful, New Hampshire

Lifting the Burden

May 2001

had been sober in AA for two years when I went to a meeting and admitted I felt ashamed of being an alcoholic. The feedback I got was extensive and helpful, and something one fellow said to me really clicked. "It sounds as if you're ready for Step Five," he said.

I was between sponsors at the time, so I asked a woman who attended one of my regular meetings if she'd hear my Fifth Step. Using all I had learned about Step Four in the meetings, I set about writing my inventory.

Searching and fearless it was, as I proceeded to write pages that unearthed memories I'd long buried. And along with my past history, I realized I wanted to be rid of a resentment against someone I'd been carrying since getting sober. I had tried to pray for the person and to let go of the resentment, but each day my anger toward this person still simmered. I knew I was finally ready to be rid of the resentment when I admitted it was hindering my progress toward sobriety and peace.

When I finished my Step Four writing, a friend suggested that I not let too much time go by between writing my inventory and sharing it. So one cold February day in 1990, I sat at her table and read my inventory.

Before I started, however, she offered some important guidance: "Remember that our Higher Power is also here listening" and "You can trust that nothing you say will leave this room." That second statement was especially helpful because if anything was an exercise in trust for me, it was this experience.

As I read my inventory, I was sure she'd be shocked or judgmental. What a relief to encounter only understanding and acceptance. I felt my shame melt away. When I finished, she said, "The things you've talked about today are over and no longer a part of you. If you do another Step Four and Five, it won't be on what you've addressed now, for that's gone."

I left her home that day feeling relieved of a huge burden and also cleansed. Several days later, I realized I hadn't once thought of the person I'd resented so much. This was a miracle. Through Step Five, God had removed my shame about being an alcoholic as well as the resentment I'd harbored for so long. And that freedom still exists, years later.

Teresa P.
Syracuse, New York

As Real as I Can Be

May 2003

I once heard at a meeting that Step Five was about integrity. By that time in my sobriety, I had realized that I didn't always understand the correct meaning of words, so I looked it up. Here are some definitions that helped me understand the word integrity in regard to the Fifth Step:

Integrity: honesty, sincerity

Honest: being free from deceit; genuine

Genuine: being what I really am

Sincere: being the same on the inside as I am in outward appearance

So for me, integrity, as it applies to the Fifth Step, is the state of being "real"—being the same on the outside as I am on the inside.

My Fifth Step was the closest I'd ever gotten to being that real to another person. More than just a confession of my faults, it was also a way of showing someone my feelings and fears. I still find today that I need to strive to be as real as I can be. Perfect integrity all the time is something that I may never achieve, but it's an ideal that I must be willing to work toward.

The program tells me that in order to recover I must be willing to develop a manner of living that demands rigorous honesty. So when I retire at night, I ask myself: Is there something that I should discuss with another person at once? What do I not want to share? Do I feel any guilt? Am I worried about something? Fearful? What was my thought-life like today?

These questions spur me to talk to someone. The more I share, the more I live "in integrity"; and the more I live in integrity, the more at peace I am with myself, and the more useful I can be to God and my fellows.

Lisa N.
Enumclaw, Washington

Ugly Words

May 2010

One day, I was preparing for my Fifth Step with my sponsor, D.G., who lives in California. We were going to do it via an internet phone system, because I live in Japan and it was difficult to see him directly.

Fifteen months had passed since my last formal inventory. Originally we planned to do my Fifth Step two months prior to this, when I went to California, but during my stay, his mother, who had been sick for a year, passed away. So I returned to Japan with my inventory sheets remaining unopened, and I rescheduled my Fifth Step. In the interim, some new troubles had come up and I was emotionally confused, so I seriously needed to clean up myself.

One hour before the new starting time we had planned, D.G. called me with bad news. His sponsor (my grandsponsor), B.M., had been killed in a motorcycle crash. D.G. was very much in shock and asked me if we could postpone my Fifth Step again. It was also shocking for me, but I could not accept it, because I was in a spiritual crisis. I should have been sorry for him losing his mother and sponsor within such a short period of time, but I was not. Instead I remembered it was the second postponement of my Step and I said, "God does not want me to take the Steps." D.G. got angry and said, "That is a very self-centered statement. You are not a victim." I knew it, but I could not control my words. I was thinking only about my pain. He said, "I'll call you later." After hanging up, I regretted that I said such an ugly thing, and I cried. I had been in contact with B.M., my grandsponsor, many times, and I loved him. However, I resented his passing because it interrupted my inventory—I hated that part of myself.

D.G. called me back a short while later and said, "Let's do as we planned." I was surprised. He told me that some of his friends had recommended that he hear my inventory and get out of himself. He also said that B.M. would have told him to go help a suffering alcoholic. His voice was very calm—different from in the previous call. He said, "Now I can concentrate on your inventory."

We started the Fifth Step with the Serenity Prayer. It took us seven hours over a two-day period. Through that process, I felt relieved. I came back to the grace of God. I was full of gratitude to my sponsor and the people around him for helping me.

After finishing my Fifth Step, I went to a meeting, where the topic was the Fifth Tradition: "Each group has but one primary purpose—to carry its message to the alcoholic who still suffers." I recognized that I was a suffering alcoholic who had received the message, and I had to pass it on.

I'm happy I was saved from my crisis and that sanity had returned. Although I don't like to find excessive meanings in someone's death, I learned AA's love through this loss.

T. S.
Japan

STEP SIX

"Were entirely ready to have God remove all these defects of character."

R endered white as snow, all our defects removed? Don't count on it. "So far as we know, it is nowhere on the record that God has completely removed from any human being all his natural drives," says the essay on Step Six in the "Twelve and Twelve."

"The Sixth is not dramatic. There are no enthusiastic witnesses to rush up and shake one's hand. It's a rather solitary affair and hence seems simple," writes a Grapevine contributor in 1980. "The Sixth Step means facing ourselves, and that is often more difficult than being honest with another person. I have found it difficult to lie to others but still easy to lie to myself. When I say, all too swiftly, 'Of course, I'm willing to change,' I now ask myself, 'Really? Who's kidding who?'"

The Step has proven a real eye-opener for many AAs. "I had spent my entire life in a world of selfishness, dishonesty and fear. I had no idea how often I had been self-seeking and dishonest. I played the victim, blaming my environment, my childhood and other people—anything except the real problem, my self-centeredness," writes another author in a 2009 story.

"Step Six represents to me the beginning of a drastic change in myself and a new perspective. Change is scary, even if it promises a better life," she writes. "I do not have the option of holding on to any of my defects. I must be willing to get rid of everything."

And yet, the "Twelve and Twelve" reminds us, it's about progress. Only Step One can be practiced with perfection. "The remaining Steps state perfect ideals," the book says. "We shall have to be content with patient improvement."

See other AAs' writings on Step Six in the pages that follow.

Wrinkles in My Ego

October 1979

S tep Six says, "Were entirely ready to have God remove all these defects of character." How to be entirely ready has been quite a puzzler for me. I have to keep in mind that the Step does not say, "I tinkered with my personality till I became perfect." First of all, I am not sure what perfect is; and second, when it comes to ironing out the wrinkles in my ego, I am about as clever as a gorilla repairing a wristwatch.

The first thing I have to keep in mind is that God does the removing, as well as deciding what is to be removed. So many of my difficulties were caused by the misapplication of God-given virtues that if I tried to sort them out, I would very likely throw out much of the wheat with the chaff. But, after twenty years of trying to become entirely ready for God to do his work, I can honestly say it sure is worth the effort.

At one time or another, many of us feel insecure, inadequate and uncertain. Somehow, we just aren't very enthusiastic about the present. As of today, I am quite sure what not to do for this state of affairs. I used to resort to a form of liquid courage that seemed to be just what I needed.

For me today, the process of becoming ready to have God remove these defects of character starts with being where it is happening—at meetings! If we ask for God's guidance and go about our business as though we were going to get it—we will. I also believe that we should be active in seeking God's help and passive in accepting his guidance.

Perhaps, one of the next things to remember is that, since I have been mixed-up for several decades, it would not be realistic for me to expect to come up smelling like Albert Schweitzer overnight. "Though the mills of God grind slowly, yet they grind exceeding small." I have to tell myself: Stay sober and wait.

It is very difficult to steer a parked car and make much progress toward any destination. I try to get moving by using what I have. When I first came to AA, I was so far gone, I couldn't remember a phone number long enough to dial it, so I had to write it down. I was not stable enough to hold a good job, so I took a mediocre job. In fact, I had five jobs after I sobered up, and each paid less than the previous one. You might say I had a very promising future behind me. The sixth job finally paid off, and I got back to my trade. I had to use what I had. In short, I had to be going somewhere before I could be guided.

These are some of the things I have learned along the way from the people in AA. I have also seen people who have grasped the program hang on in spite of tremendous odds, such as slow death by cancer or sudden loss of loved ones by accident. Whatever the character defects of these people might have been, drinking was not among them. They stuck to the program.

God as I understand him does not cheat anyone. I don't pretend to know how, when, or where the score is evened up, but I am certain that it always is.

J. B.

Rochester, New York

Are We Really Willing to Change?

December 1980

The First Step was a cinch for me. I had run out of options, and the results of my drinking had been devastating; so self-debate about drinking simply didn't exist. I knew I couldn't drink safely. I did the First Step at the moment I entered a hospital for detoxification, and I have never questioned it since.

It then took several weeks to get to the Second Step, but it became apparent that I hadn't stopped drinking on my own. A Higher Power had obviously intervened, so the Third Step was understandable and necessary.

My sponsor pushed, shoved and tugged, and I eventually did the Fourth and Fifth Steps. From that point onward, I made immense progress. Even the Ninth Step was faced with resolution and courage. I made the appropriate amends and experienced the feeling of liberation that my sponsor had promised. The other Steps were the logical extension of the program for me. I became active in Twelfth Step work and enjoyed the rewards.

Still, something was missing. There remained lingering feelings of vague discontent. The personality flaws I had uncovered in doing the Fourth and Fifth Steps had diminished—but were still there. And they started up the same old process that had produced feelings I had when drinking—impatience, irascibility, quick temper, and an unforgiving attitude toward others. I didn't like the way I felt, so I had dinner with my sponsor and discussed my situation frankly with him.

He gave me one of his knowing smiles, but said nothing. "Well," I demanded, "what's your solution to this problem?"

"You really think you've done all the Steps, don't you?" he asked. I assured him, somewhat indignantly, that I had. Hadn't I done the Fourth and Fifth with him? Had he not seen my Twelfth Step activity with his own eyes? Wasn't he aware of how faithfully—in my mind—I was doing the Tenth Step?

"All very true," he said, "but what about the Sixth Step?"

That came like a bolt from the blue. Of course, I was willing to change and have my Higher Power remove my defects of character, wasn't I? ... Was I?

If I was sincerely willing to change, why did I remain so much the same? I realized that I had been paying lip service to the Sixth Step. Compared to most of the other Steps, the Sixth is apparently simple. I believed this, because no overt action seemed required. There is none of the dramatic confrontation that exists when we do the Ninth Step, nor is there the feeling of accomplishment that comes with the Twelfth. The Sixth is not dramatic. There are no enthusiastic witnesses to rush up and shake one's hand. It's a rather solitary affair and hence seems simple.

The Sixth Step means facing ourselves, and that is often more difficult than being honest with another person. I have found it difficult to lie to others but still easy to lie to myself. When I say, all too swiftly, "Of course, I'm willing to change," I now ask myself, "Really? Who's kidding who?" The fact that I am now questioning my willingness to change has increased my ability to be increasingly willing. I simply don't take the process as lightly as I did before. I can't learn anything unless I'm sincerely willing to learn. Nor will making myself promises to change have any significance until the willingness factor is developed.

My sponsor intervened again with a few of his pointed questions. "You played football in college, didn't you?" he asked—knowing full well that I had. He reminded me that I had told him I absolutely hated the practice, "getting all those lumps and bruises for no good reason." And he also reminded me how I had said I loved the actual game, especially the applause when I did something very well.

"You know," he said, "no one gets all excited about the practice. It has no flash to it. It's the game that counts. But a good game performance requires hard practice. And the Sixth Step can be compared with football practice. If you're going to continue to make progress in the program and with the other eleven Steps, you have to really work on the Sixth Step. Don't stand around on one foot waiting for applause. There won't be any. But you'll play a far better game."

What my sponsor told me carries an important moral lesson. It's one I'm working diligently to learn, because I now—finally—see the true value of the Sixth Step.

R.B.
Manhattan, New York

Don't Skip Over Six

December 1993

M y sponsor has been sober, quite contentedly, for eleven years and I respect his experience. So when he talks, I listen.

"Work the Steps," he told me, "They're the essence of Alcoholics Anonymous. That's why people in isolated places can successfully get sober and stay sober. They work the Steps."

Totally convinced, I went ahead on the Steps and actually did some minor Twelfth Step work before I had reached my second anniversary in AA. I made amends to some people who had every reason to never forgive me. Two people did not and probably never will. But I felt better having taken the action.

Not too long ago, feeling depressed and discouraged, I phoned my sponsor to see if he could have dinner with me and listen to my whining. We met and I skated all around the subject. We talked about football until dessert when he asked, "Don't you think that it's about time you get down to the reason for this meeting—over and above how the Giants are doing this season?"

There was no way to delay my complaints although the depression had lifted to some degree. I blurted out, "You damn near promised me a 'new and better life' if I did the Steps and so far my life isn't all that much improved."

He gave me a look of slight annoyance and said, "You're misquoting me. I never said a word about 'doing' the Steps. I particularly stressed the need to work the Steps. That doesn't mean tap dancing around the tough things. It means being realistic. It means making serious structural changes in the way you act and the way you think. And you missed one Step completely. At least it hasn't registered on you."

"What the hell do you mean? Which Step have I ignored?"

His answer rang in my head: "The Sixth."

A swift rebuttal was forthcoming. "Of course I'm willing to change. What makes you conclude that I'm not?"

My sponsor said, "How about your constant procrastination? You told me you'd return a book I lent you five months ago and you still have the book. So think about procrastination, a lingering fault."

And he continued, "What about your tendency to project? To envision the worst? The way you holler long before you're hurt? Remember how you sweated out a dental appointment to get root canal work? You lived in misery for two weeks before you had it done. Afterward, remember, you boasted that it was 'a piece of cake.'"

Nor was the man through with me. He said, "What about the so-called 'harmless white lies'? You still telling those? The answer to that is yes. Do you want a specific example? I overheard you saying, 'The last time I was in Paris.' You know and I know you've been there only once. But the way you phrased it, you wanted your audience to conclude you fly to Paris for weekends.

"So cut the bull and level with yourself. You haven't worked the Sixth Step. You know why? It looks so simple. It's so easy to skip lightly over it. But the Fourth and Fifth Steps—your personal inventory—are meaningless unless and until you get the guts and honesty to do something about the faults. Lecture concluded."

The no-holds-barred tone of my sponsor's critique hit me hard. I was stunned, but it was just what I needed. If you think the Sixth Step is a snap and that there's nothing to it, I suggest this: imagine yourself in my place at dinner with my sponsor. Imagine he spoke directly about your character defects. Would you be sanguine, smug and self-satisfied?

Ralph B.

New York, New York

Making Room to Grow Up

June 1997

Were entirely ready to have God remove all these defects of character." So reads Step Six. After the guilt and remorse of my last drunk had faded, I didn't think this Step had any application in my life. Now that I was no longer drinking I wasn't a bad person. Character defects? I couldn't see where I had any. My character defects were hidden behind all those hurts and injustices I'd saved up through the years and which I regularly brought out and relived with all the original emotion. Not only that, I accumulated any and every new hurt, real or imagined. In fact I took a kind of perverse pleasure from feeling sad and self-pitying. I was giving power to people who were long gone. Then I realized that these people gave me my favorite excuses for why I did what I did or couldn't do what I should have done. I used them to justify my actions and blamed them for my failures. Every time something went wrong in my life or I failed to live up to some responsibility, I took out the list of abuses I'd suffered and used it as an excuse. I became very adept at hiding my guilt behind these real or imagined hurts. I was a chronic victim.

The problem with blaming my frustrations and failures on what others did to me is that it kept me small. I stayed a little boy trapped in a man's body—a self-centered, selfish little boy who expected people to live up to his fantasies of them and got hurt when they didn't cater to every want and whim.

Although I had made a Third Step decision, I couldn't really turn my life and will over to my Higher Power because it didn't belong to me. Unknowingly, over the years, I'd turned my will over to all those people whom I felt had injured me in some way.

Fortunately I reached a point where I was choking on all this garbage. With the help of my Higher Power and the AA program, I chose to grow up. It was about time! I opened up that imaginary closet in my mind where I kept these well-nurtured hurts and tossed them into my past, where they belonged. Into this newly cleaned-out space, I started storing my goals and the hopes and dreams of what I wanted to achieve in life. Now instead of looking backward into the dreariness of my past, I'm looking forward to a bright future because I've finally taken responsibility for my life.

Ron D.

Canaan, Connecticut

As Long as I Stay Willing

June 2009

S tep Six is about having the willingness to hand over my defects to God. After working Step Five with my sponsor, I asked myself if I was really ready for things to change. I had spent my entire life in a world of selfishness, dishonesty and fear. I had no idea how often I had been self-seeking and dishonest. I played the victim, blaming my environment, my childhood and other people—anything except the real problem, my self-centeredness. This insanity landed me in the hospital after trying to end my life. It was eye-opening to find the root of my troubles. I was miserable but I found comfort in the pain and it was all I could relate to. For me, drinking was a great validation for my self-hatred. It was the only answer I had.

Step Six represents to me the beginning of a drastic change in myself and a new perspective. Change is scary, even if it promises a better life. Yet in the beginning, I said I would go to any lengths, and my idea of living almost killed me.

I do not have the option of holding on to any of my defects. I must be willing to get rid of everything.

Taking these leaps of faith and trusting God has brought me much relief. I know that everything will fall into place as long as I stay willing.

Dawn M.

Watsonville, California

I'm No Saint!

June 2009

Sometimes sitting home taking time off sounds like a deserved reward. I "need" some time just for me, don't I? Don't I do enough? Why do I always have to be the one to make sacrifices? No one else has to. My group couldn't get along without me, you know. Of course, if they would only do things the way I suggest ... if only they would listen to me ... if only I had more control around here and more money than I am currently making and a different relationship (someone who really understands and loves me), then I could finally relax and begin to enjoy my sobriety.

I get so angry when I see people slacking off on their Step work, service work, their commitments. It's a wonder they stay sober. You should see the way some people treat their friends and families. I have to stay away from most of them just to keep from losing it!

Oh my. A little righteous anger is better than a double espresso. I get all revved up—but with nowhere to go except out, if I'm not careful. When I start thinking along these lines, sooner or later I think of Step Six and mainly two things: "Would I rather be right, or would I rather be happy?" and "The truth will set you free."

The truth is, when I begin to focus on the failings of others, I become restless, irritable and discontented. What seem to be my finely tuned mind and my "innate sense of fairness" are in reality my character defects judging the world and finding it lacking.

Step Six is simple in the way Einstein's theory of relativity is simple—easy to say, difficult to explain. The simple version is: Looking at my moral inventory, am I willing to ask God to remove the defects in my character that caused pain, suffering, longstanding resentments and guilt? Of course. End of Step.

Easy, all right, until Step Twelve, where we "practice these principles in all our affairs." Oh, but what about having just a little bit of personal pride in my Step work, service work or sobriety date? What about judging others in the Fellowship or family members? What about envying the "easy" sobriety others seem to have? Others get away with only one meeting a week, or less. I have to make up for lost time, you know. I need to work more hours, obtain a better position, make more money, acquire the things I denied myself or gave away.

Ideas that sound really good at the time are sometimes surrounded by motives that are selfish, self-centered, dishonest, self-seeking, inconsiderate or based on fear. If I can't see the truth, I can't make appropriate decisions. I won't be able to "intuitively know" how to deal with situations. The world will continue to baffle and control me.

Without working the Steps in order, praying, listening for answers in meetings, studying the literature, doing service and talking with my sponsor, I couldn't have figured anything out, let alone felt good about it. I'd have second-guessed myself into a standstill and mounted up so many resentments in the Fellowship that I'd have talked myself into running away from the only good thing I'd stumbled onto in decades—the one place that was sincerely trying to help me save my life.

The program and the Fellowship of Alcoholics Anonymous has taught me more about myself than 10 years of psychiatric work experience; a couple years of therapy; and thousands of dollars' worth of booze, self-help books and women's magazines ever did.

The idea that when I find fault with you, the problem is in me is not just a clever platitude. It is one more step toward true freedom and happiness. When I begin to look where the answer really is—inside of me—I get a sense of "rightness" when I speak or hear the truth. Step Six helps me develop a sense of intuition that I can truly count on.

Now, I'd love to have people believe that having taken the Sixth Step, I am free from all those nasty character defects. Or at least, that if I ever did have thoughts of pride, envy, jealousy, etc., I would recognize these for what they were and immediately become ready to have God remove them. But, some of you know me, and, those who don't, if they are real alcoholics, are not likely to be fooled with all of this "saintly" talk. I am no saint. I'm not even always "willing to grow along spiritual lines." But I have changed. As a result of working the Steps, I am not the same person I was when I half-heartedly began to just go to some meetings. And the change is good. Definitely. So, on the good days, it is kind of exciting to build my relationship with God, through the Sixth Step.

On the bad days, if I can just remember the glimmer of hope I found when I first recognized the truth about myself, I can pray for willingness and I can believe it will come.

Sue H.
Fort Myers, Florida

My Armor

June 2010

While I had no problem admitting I was an alcoholic, I didn't believe I was the kind of alcoholic who joined AA, the kind who had to stop drinking altogether, who could never take another drink. "One day at a time," they said. But I knew what that meant: "One day at a time ... for the rest of your life." Oh, no, not me, buddy! I was pretty sure I was the kind who cut down. You know, a mild case.

My plan was to take a look at these famous Twelve Steps (whatever they were), analyze them and decide which of them I might apply to seriously cutting down. My drinking had admittedly gotten out of hand. Since I had no intention of stopping entirely, I surely wouldn't need all twelve.

A couple of the Steps seemed to be unnecessary. Six and Eight, for instance, were preparation for Steps that followed, and had been stuck in there to make an even dozen, no doubt. Step Six especially, I thought, was a useless space saver. "Were entirely ready to have God remove all these defects of character."

Who wouldn't want to have their defects removed? I'd like to be a nice guy. I'd like to have people think well of me. Maybe it would help me to keep a job, maintain a friendship ... or have a second date with the same girl.

The problem was that I hadn't identified any defects. Little did I know that I had developed, cultivated and come to depend on an army of character defects. They weren't even pests to me. They were more like beloved pets that I fed and nurtured.

Arrogance, for example, was self-confidence. I'm not lustful—I'm romantic by nature. You might call me selfish—I call it frugal. You call it gluttony—I call it lunch. If I'm intolerant, critical or judgmental of others, I call it being ruthlessly honest and painfully frank. As for my own dishonesty, I denied it. "I pride myself on my personal integrity." In other words, I lied!

When, after months of attending AA meetings, I finally did stop drinking, got a sponsor and decided to apply the Steps to my life, I discovered that taking the Twelve Steps is an entirely different experience than reading them or hearing them read.

Step Six is an extremely significant part of the process. In fact, I've come to think of the Sixth Step as the "gateway Step."

After taking Step Five, I had a list of people to whom I owed amends. I would deal with them at Steps Eight and Nine. The list at hand now was the list of my character defects, my shortcomings. These were the manifestations of self that had placed me in a position to be hurt and to hurt others.

These were the elements of my personal armor I had gathered over my life. I put them on and wore them as if into battle. They may have been heavy and awkward, but I believed that they protected me.

Step Six suggests I place them all on the table and let God sort them out, ask God to decide which I need and don't need. There may be things I consider shortcomings that my Higher Power has some use for, just as there may be things I consider virtues that need to be cleared away for my spiritual well-being.

My meditation was once interrupted by what I considered some worldly and less than spiritual thoughts. I was so irritated by this that I shared it with my wife and exclaimed, "I need to ask God to remove my lust." Her response was, "Don't you dare!"

Evidently she had some use for such distractions and considered them beneficial.

On the other hand, as an artist, I have long considered pride in my work a necessary tool of the trade. And though pride has its usefulness in craftsmanship, it is a total liability in spiritual matters. The Big Book refers to the "leveling of our pride."

That doesn't mean evening it out like we might "level" a sand lot, it means like they level an old building to build a new one in its place. It has to be destroyed.

The Seventh Step Prayer says, "I am now willing that you should have all of me, good and bad. I pray that you now remove from me every single defect of character which stands in the way of my usefulness to you and my fellows."

So Step Six may be the greatest act of courage in the whole twelve-step process: a total act of faith. I have to trust that God will see the big picture and make the right choices. Funny thing is, without all that armor, it's a lot easier to move. In fact, I feel like dancing through the rest of the Steps.

Doug R.
Tujunga, California

STEP SEVEN

"Humbly asked Him to remove our shortcomings."

The chief activator of our defects has been self-centered fear—primarily fear that we would lose something we already possessed or would fail to get something we demanded," says the "Twelve and Twelve." "No peace was to be had unless we could find a means of reducing these demands." This begins to happen with Step Seven. We begin to move out from ourselves, toward others and toward God, and we begin to have moments of real peace of mind.

"I actually thought the Step implied a goal of perfection which I believed impossible to achieve, but one that I should try to reach," writes the author of a 1957 Grapevine story. "When my many abortive attempts to perfect myself had failed (as they were bound to do) I sank back deeper into the very defect I should have avoided—guilt."

The writer, with more reflection and time sober, later realizes, "I don't want to become perfect or God-like. I simply want to become more human. ... I am simply trying to throw off all the garbage of hostility and resentments that has rotted my insides, and all the guilt that has weighed me down these many years, and the fear that has paralyzed my personality into rigid habit-patterns. These are the defects that impede or block me."

"The whole emphasis of Step Seven is on humility," the "Twelve and Twelve" says. "We now ought to be willing to try humility in seeking the removal of our other shortcomings just as we did when we admitted we were powerless over alcohol."

Little Surrenders

August 1982

About two years ago, I made a fortuitous discovery while experiencing a disturbing episode during my recovery. As a result, the Seventh Step became my tool for everyday coping and living. The emotional impact of this happening was like that of finding a new religion—the feelings of exhilaration persisted for several weeks.

Immediately prior to the discovery, I had worked myself into a near frenzy over distressing evidence of my inability to handle my own financial affairs. My income was adequate, and I knew there was no good reason for running out of money. Of course, this was not the first time it had happened. Once more, I had yielded to impulses to buy things, and my expenditures for the month had far exceeded available funds—or, for that matter, prospects for borrowing money to cover the deficit. My carefully laid budget plans had again proved fruitless.

I was very displeased with myself. Feelings of inadequacy rose. I soon began to doubt that I had any ability at all to cope with life. In a matter of hours, I became despondent and almost desperate. At that point, the thought struck me that I had indeed uncovered a serious character defect. I had never seen this problem in quite that light before, and I knew I had better turn to God for help.

I was sitting in a room all by myself. So I fell to my knees—literally, as AA co-founder Dr. Bob always counseled newcomers—and said aloud, "God, help me with this problem, I simply can't handle it." It was really a Seventh Step and also a surrender experience. Almost immediately, I felt relief from the intense anxiety that built up within me. My mind began to clear. Soon, new thoughts helped me to extricate myself from the dilemma. Weeks later, I developed techniques to prevent me from again committing serious errors of that sort.

A couple of days after the initial discovery, I paused to consider two surrender experiences of mine during my early days in AA. The first had opened the door to wholehearted acceptance of the AA program, resulting in the disappearance of my craving for alcohol in a matter of hours. The second occurred much later and led to a resolution of a serious inner conflict that had stood in the way of reliable sobriety. I realized that although the recent event had been less crucial than the first two, it was still very important.

Furthermore, I saw that this Step approach could be applied whenever I reached a similar impasse of my own making, whether it be of outer circumstances or inner emotions. Whenever I find myself uptight, I fall on my knees, literally or figuratively—depending on my surroundings—and ask God's help. It comes easier to me now. In fact, during the past two years, my life has been marked by a series of these "little surrenders."

As the months have passed and surrender has followed surrender, I have come to a higher insight concerning this application of the Seventh Step. It is this: If I were able to retain the attitude that I achieve during the hours immediately following these crisis experiences, life would be continuously euphoric—I would forever be immersed in the kind of feelings I achieved for only brief periods with alcohol at the beginning. Let's call it a "surrendered attitude." It is the avenue to "the peace ... which passeth all understanding." I perceived that whatever happens to me is not nearly so important as the way I look at the happening—the way I feel about it. We really do carry our worlds within ourselves.

D.J.

Columbus, Ohio

Mail Call: Step Seven

November 1949

What are our shortcomings? Was it just drunkenness? No, that was just one of the many other character defects with which we are burdened. Among them are conceit, arrogance, selfishness, dishonesty, intolerance and worst of all the searing and caustic tongue with which we whiplashed ourselves and others, some of whom have tried to help us.

How can we expect God as we understand Him to remove these shortcomings when we are too small and prideful to admit them? These things must be brought out into the open, must be admitted and then exposed to the cleansing effect of the sunlight of humility and honesty.

A humble person in true humility does this without reservations, he doesn't do it partially, he does it wholly, even though it might hurt. Why? For the same reason that a surgeon excises a cancer totally—he takes out the whole evil mess because then there is no chance of a recurrence. Why shouldn't we do the same? It takes a little more effort and is a lot more painful to our ego, but the cure is more apt to be permanent.

The expression of true humility is the willingness to serve others without expectation of reward, prestige or recognition for our services to them. It should be done in a spirit of cheerfulness and joy.

We must at all times be willing to subordinate ourselves to a Power greater than ourselves. We should neither by thought nor expression be critical of others or their opinions. We must be big enough to give the other fellow the right of expression, give credit where credit is due, be a doer instead of a critical wisher. In short be of AA and not just in it.

This above all: to thine own self be true, And it must follow, as the night the day, Thou canst not then be false to any man.

Ernie
Chicago, Illinois

Food for the Journey

July 2007

I used to draw a blank when I heard the word "humility." Or perhaps not a blank so much as confusion. For me, to be humble was to have, as one dictionary put it, "a feeling of inferiority and insignificance," to feel inadequate and unworthy. The dictionary linked being humble with being humiliated, which in turn pointed to being dishonored, disgraced, and shamed. Its synonyms included "meekness," "submissiveness," and "lowliness."

I didn't want humility! Shame and feelings of inferiority haunted me not only in active alcoholism but even before, in a childhood marked by various forms of abuse and neglect. I was the kid who failed in sports, a member of the out-group, and a loner who would lose himself in a book because he couldn't fit in with the guys. In a couple of places, the Big Book spoke of the importance of ego-deflation. I understood that there were people with a grandiose opinion of themselves who could profit from a good helping of ego-deflation—but I came to the rooms feeling empty and unworthy.

So, even though Step Seven began with the word "humbly," to me, humility did not seem to be of any great importance to recovery. In the first 164 pages of the Big Book, humility and being humble are mentioned only a handful of times.

Many people, I suspect, have come into AA sharing my idea of what humility is, or at least something close to it. And, it did not seem to be a preferred topic for discussion in the meetings I attended. On those rare occasions when the topic did come up (usually when the discussion was about Step Seven), people often spoke about some event in their lives that made them feel inferior or foolish in front of others. Most of the time, humility was seen as humiliation. Occasionally, it was linked to gratitude.

At one meeting, a man spoke eloquently about how he had gotten his family, job and self-respect back; his health, wealth, and a cluster of good friends—all of which made him feel "humbled." To me, it sounded more like gratitude.

Something was missing; or rather, I was missing something. In the "Twelve and Twelve," the whole emphasis of the Step is on humility. Bill W. wrote that it is "a clear recognition of what and who we really are, followed by a sincere attempt to become what we could be." It is "a healer of pain" and "the avenue to the true freedom of the spirit," which can bring us to a "great turning point in our lives." In fact, he continued, "the attainment of greater humility is the foundation principle of each of AA's Twelve Steps." There is no "humble pie" or "groveling despair" in any of this!

Bill's reflections represented humility in a way that was vastly different from what I had originally thought, but I was still puzzled. How exactly was humility linked to self-recognition? How could it heal pain or bring spiritual freedom? How could it be "the foundation principle" of all the Steps? I had already been through the Steps a couple of times, but I wasn't aware of humility being a part of each of them. I later realized that humility-as-humiliation was still clouding my thinking.

Then there was the day that the meeting focused on powerlessness. A teenage son was acting up, rebelling, drinking and doing drugs; his mother was desperately trying to control him. But despite her efforts, his behavior had not changed. It was obvious to many that nothing she could do would change him. It was a contest of wills and she was losing.

I remembered my own troubles with my youngest son, who had severed relations with me long after I had sobered up. None of my efforts could win him back. I spent hours with my sponsor being reminded that I was powerless over other people, hours in which he encouraged me to work on myself and to focus on staying open to my son, ready to welcome him into my life after he had found his own way back to me.

My futile attempts to bring about what was beyond my power had brought me only anger and frustration, the very pain the woman at the meeting was suffering over her son. It was then that I had a sudden moment of clarity. Humility is not humiliation, though humiliation could bring us to it. It was not gratitude, though humility could bring us gratitude. For me, humility relates to power: It is the recognition and acceptance of the limits of my own power. I therefore began to understand that humility was indeed the foundation of all the Steps, and so could be a healer of pain, a way to spiritual freedom, and a turning point in our lives.

Each of the Steps asks humility of us. It was grudging humility, but humility nevertheless, that led me to seek help for my alcoholism: a turning point in my life. It was humility that led me to ask someone to sponsor me. And it is humility that keeps me going to meetings. Each of these actions is saying, "I need your help." As a result, my healing progresses. It is humility when I ask my sponsor and others for help in seeing myself as I really am, an important beginning of spiritual freedom from my defects. It is humility when I allow myself to be taught how to make amends, thereby healing damaged relationships. It is humility again when I call on God to relieve me of my defects, to show me his will, and to empower me to do it. I turn to others for strength to bear the pain, sorrow, and disappointment that are an inevitable part of all human lives. Each of these is a way of saying that, on my own, I could not do those things that are so necessary for my spiritual growth. This is why we say, "This is a 'we' program."

The simple word "we" stands at the entrance to the Steps, reminding me that my power is limited. It reminds me that it is through God's help and the help of others that I gain the strength to work toward the spiritual awakening that is the final goal of the Twelve Steps. "We" begins our journey; humility is the food that strengthens us on our way.

Jamie C.
West Henrietta, New York

Ham on Wry

May 1996

A businessman working on his Seventh Step complained to his sponsor, "I don't get it. I prayed for humility and the Board of Directors forced me out. So I became vice president of another big operation. I prayed for humility again and got fired from that job, too! What should I do?" The sponsor said, "Pray for something else."

The Rose

July 1991

In January, I celebrated my seventh birthday in Alcoholics Anonymous. As I look back over the year, I realize it was the very best year ever in my sobriety, for it was linked inextricably with the Seventh Step and the absolute necessity for me to keep on changing. As Dr. Silkworth states in the Big Book, unless the alcoholic can "experience an entire psychic change there is very little hope of his recovery." Frequently last year, I was confronted with the pain of change. One day last week, I found myself confronted with yet another painful defect.

At first, I did what I usually do at such times. I tried to rationalize the defect away, then tried to blame it on somebody else and finally began to say to myself, "This I shall never give up." That's when I knew I was in real trouble. At about this time, I went to a meeting that was on exactly what I needed to hear—Step Seven. As I listened to my friends share their practical experience with this Step, I became increasingly aware that I didn't want to give up this particular defect because I was afraid—afraid of what might become of me, afraid of what God might change me into. What if I didn't like it? As I heard one of my friends refer to the "psychic change," my fear and defiance increased. But I began to listen more carefully.

When my turn came to talk, I found myself sharing with the group my first real understanding of the Seventh Step. It had occurred during my third year of sobriety. I had been figuring out Steps Six and Seven and working hard on them for over a year and had gotten absolutely nowhere. My sponsor, realizing that I was stuck, asked me to speak on these Steps at a Friday night meeting. I spent the rest of that week in a state of semi-panic, realizing that I knew all the words but had been unable to practice the Steps due to my inordinate fear of change.

Early Friday morning when I arrived at the high school where I taught, I was met at the back door by two boys who were in my eleventh grade class. They were both grinning from ear to ear with a great surprise they had planned. All of my students had been attending an arts festival that week and were enjoying the challenge of finding a "poem" to bring back to English class in order to earn extra credit. I had received all sorts of "poems"—from weeds and wild flowers to a sublime strawberry crepe, whipped cream and all! These two students were eager to walk me to class to show me their "poem" before everybody else arrived.

When we arrived in the classroom, I saw a huge yellow helium balloon on my desk. The boys had tied the string inside a small vase that sat on my desk, and the balloon floated there like a bright, happy exclamation mark. On the balloon they had written some sort of ridiculous poem which they knew would make me laugh. Then one of the students, Larry, pulled a long florist's pin from behind his back and held it out toward me. "Pop it, Mrs. E.," he said.

I recoiled. I couldn't. I hate to pop balloons. It scares me, and I usually scream. "Pop it, Mrs. E." Larry was insistent. I continued to refuse, giving all sorts of great excuses and reasons. "Pop it, Mrs. E." I laughed, I teased, I cajoled. But one of Larry's greatest assets was his stubborn persistence, and I knew we would stand there forever or at least until I popped the balloon. Finally I took the pin, put one hand over an ear, closed my eyes, held my breath, and popped the balloon. I didn't scream. I opened my eyes. Concealed inside the now disintegrated balloon was a long-stemmed red rose. I have no idea how they put it inside the balloon. I felt my eyes fill with joy, and I hugged Larry.

At last I understood the Seventh Step. I am so full of hot air, I am afraid to let God pop my balloon of pride and fear. I am afraid of what I will find. But that day, God showed me—an American Beauty rose. That night as I shared the story with a roomful of drunks, I looked at all of them and realized I was looking at God's garden of roses. Again I wept for joy. I realized that I, too, am part of his garden.

I have really learned only one thing since that day. I will not see my own rose. I must trust God for that as I continue to practice Steps Six and Seven. But my faith in this process of change increases as I look upon my fellow drunks and watch them blossom. I trust they are a reflection of what happens to me when I let go and let God.

Annie E.
Oklahoma

Rock Bottom

July 2009

Monday morning: My sponsor has asked me to make a list of my character defects so that we can do Steps Six and Seven when we meet later in the day. It has been weeks since I've met with her to do Step work, and I've been wallowing in my character defects since I finished reading her my Fifth Step. I'm anxious and frustrated. I'm angry about other issues in my life. I'm ready to get some relief and do these two Steps. Unfortunately, our schedules change and we can no longer meet. I can't hang on to these any longer, but I'm not really sure what to do.

Earlier in the week I had practiced talking to God. I definitely can admit to believing in a Higher Power, but I've always questioned whether or not she actually has any interest in me on a personal level. My sponsor has been encouraging me for months to practice praying, even if I don't think it will do anything. She also suggested writing a letter to God, allowing her to respond. It was during that assignment that I found myself having a full-blown conversation with God in my journal. In that dialogue I wrote that all I wanted to do was go throw rocks in the ocean.

So, back to Monday morning: What to do with myself now that we're not meeting? I debate a meeting, and I debate driving to the beach to throw rocks in the ocean. The beach wins. It's a drizzly, gray morning and I'm not really prepared for the weather, but I don't care. I drive to a beach that I know has lots of rocks. I climb down to the sand and sit on the rocks. I have my list of character defects and a marker, and I decide to write my defects on the rocks so I can then throw them in the water. At first I think I'll choose little rocks that are easy to throw. Then I realize my first character defect is "self-hatred" and that definitely warrants a big rock. Most of the rocks I choose are not so little. I sit and write and sit and write, until next to me I have a big pile of rocks.

I realize that the water is quite far from where I'm sitting, and I have a big pile of rocks that I'm not sure how to get there. I take the blanket I'm sitting on and bundle them up in it. I laugh when I go to pick the blanket up and realize how heavy my pile of character defects is! I am so ready to let these go. I walk to the water and empty the blanket on the sand.

I stare at the sky and I stare at the waves and just start talking and crying and asking God to please help me because I'm tired and she has to help me because I'm done trying to do it all myself. After seven-and-a-half months of sobriety, I finally stop holding onto the one last bit of self-will. I finally allow myself to really pray for God's care and protection. I recite the Seventh Step Prayer. I pick up a rock and throw it in the ocean. I pick up another rock, say the Seventh Step Prayer again and throw it in the ocean. Rock, prayer, toss, rock, prayer, toss. I look down when there are two rocks remaining and laugh. Of course they are the two biggest rocks and my two most stubborn defects. I let those go, too. And then I feel light. And I feel not so alone. And I feel God. Did I just say that? Have I just had a spiritual experience? Have I just made conscious contact with my Higher Power? The peace and quiet in my head says yes.

I walk back to where I had been sitting on the rocks. I've always heard the expression, "nature abhors a vacuum," and I ask God to fill the space that's been emptied with character assets. I ask for willingness, humility, love, honesty and compassion. I thank her for being present, for accepting my character defects. I realize the ocean is the best "God box" ever. I realize I'm no longer as afraid to be alone with my overwhelming feelings because I can just return to the water's edge and pray to God.

Praying is very new for me. I'm not really sure how to do it.

Paolina A.
Venice, California

A Lifetime Supply

July 1995

Coming into AA and finding the acceptance and love I'd sought in a bottle was a relief beyond description, but reading the Steps was a shock. Fortunately for me, my home group did not hammer the Steps into newcomers. Rather, they talked a lot about the Slogans and the need to not drink a day at a time. I needed that.

During a discussion of Step Seven, I made the statement, "If my shortcomings and character defects are removed, there will be nothing left!" I need not have feared. What I've learned since then is that I have more than a lifetime's supply of character defects. My Higher Power and I can't get rid of them all in my allotted time on this earth.

More importantly, I've learned that if I simply let go of a character defect—release it—my Higher Power will replace it with a character asset. As I release anger I find that I am friendlier. As I release hate I become more loving. As I release fear I become more secure. I don't have to go out looking for friendliness, love, security or any other trait that I desire. I just have to give up the feelings that are manifestations of my character defects and the good automatically flows into my life. And I used to think that I would become hollow without my character defects!

So, how does it work? Daily. On a daily basis I choose not to drink—or to fear, hate, be angry or indulge in any other defect that's raising its ugly head. They're all there waiting, and when given a chance they charge into the center of my life and try to take over. But when I work Step Seven I find that my life is filled with good, and people actually like to be around me—something they never did in my drinking days.

C.
Kathmandu, Nepal

Freedom from Fear

July 2000

The second-to-last paragraph of Step Seven in the "Twelve and Twelve" was the wake-up call I needed as I reluctantly began my first journey through the Steps. Finally I had found, in one sentence, the sum total of my active alcoholic life: "The chief activator of our defects has been self-centered fear—primarily fear that we would lose something we already possessed or would fail to get something we demanded."

From the day I picked up my first drink, continuing through early sobriety, fear ruled my life twenty-four hours a day. To discover that my fears were based on the selfish notion that I deserved the best that life could give me—all the while trampling on other peoples' rights and feelings—saved my sanity and life. I realized that the fear of losing people, places, or things was not only a waste of time; it caused a multitude of resentments.

My life is far from perfect, of course, but after a few twenty-four hours of sobriety and freedom from fear, I have hope and gratitude. When I remember to work the program daily, I am able to replace fear with hope.

James G.
Warwick, Rhode Island

STEP EIGHT

"Made a list of all persons we had harmed, and became willing to make amends to them all."

D efective relations with others have nearly always been the immediate cause of our woes," the essay on Step Eight in the "Twelve and Twelve" says. "We take a look backward and try to discover where we have been at fault; next we make a vigorous attempt to repair the damage we have done." As the Big Book very simply puts it: "We take the bit in our teeth."

"The first part of the Eighth Step is neither difficult to understand nor hard to go through with. As a matter of fact, if we have written out our Fourth Step inventory, we may already have the list of persons we have harmed," writes an AA in the Grapevine in 1967. "Some of the most common amends have to do with: people we owe money; wives, parents, children, relatives and friends we have mistreated; employers, employees and business associates we have harmed; people with whom we have become involved morally in an injurious manner."

The AA texts caution AAs to not be foolish martyrs when making amends: Consult with others and make sure no one else will be harmed in the process of the amends. "We should be sensible, tactful, considerate and humble without being servile or scraping," the Big Book says.

"I don't need to crawl or go on and on about how sorry I am," a 1979 Grapevine contributor writes. "I simply need to acknowledge that I was at fault and humbly ask them to pardon me. ... I need to walk tall, without false pride.

"When I go in humility and sincerely ask people to forgive me, this will remove the burden from my shoulders. They, too, may have been at fault, but I am neither their God nor their conscience. I am responsible only for myself."

The process of Step Eight is further addressed by these AAs, whose stories appeared earlier in the Grapevine.

On the Eighth Step

June 1945

I t was characteristic of many of us as alcoholics to at least attempt to perform in the grandiose manner. And in harming others we usually succeeded magnificently. So, to say that the first phase of the Eighth Step is a large order is to indulge in understatement which matches our bombastic style.

And yet, however extended be the list of those we have harmed, the fulfillment of this Step's admonition need not be a tedious nor a burdensome undertaking. In the first place, let's examine the meaning of the verb: Amend.

Webster's New International Dictionary defines it thus—"To make better, especially in character; to repair, restore; to free from faults, put right, correct, rectify ..."

There is the credo to which we of AA subscribe; the goal we hope to achieve through sobriety. It is both the manifestation of our adherence to the other 11 Steps and our performance of the Eighth itself.

The definition continues:

"... to change or modify in any way for the better; to recover from illness."

It was written for us!

We have often heard that our sobriety should be founded on "unselfish selfishness," that we should strive to avoid a lapse into drinking for the benefits we, personally, derive from abstinence. It's not sound, we have been told, to try to stay dry for the sake of a wife or a sweetheart or someone else dear to us.

When we first heard that plan of action outlined, we revolted mildly because it didn't seem to meet the specifications of true altruism. Many of us, as we entered AA, still yearned for that mystic power to "handle" alcohol and it seemed then that the Step we were taking was at least in part a gesture of devotion to some loved one. Without altruism there didn't seem to be much motive to propel us.

Of course, we soon discovered that "unselfish selfishness" was the firmest foundation for our recovery. We found, in the same way, that we try to help others, not solely through altruistic impulse, but so that we may gain strength.

The principle of "unselfish selfishness" is applicable again in the Eighth Step. We seek to identify all those we have harmed and we assume a willingness to make amends so that—recalling the definition of the word—we may "change ... for the better" and "recover from illness."

The alternative is retrogression. If we fail to "repair," we can only impair.

L.J.

Not Under the Rug

January 1967

I n approaching Step Eight for the first time, those of us who tend to fight or question various of the Steps until we become convinced they are vital to our sobriety, need reassuring on several points. We may be tempted to tell ourselves that we have done enough housecleaning in the Fourth and Fifth Steps. If we are truthful though, we will have to admit that the biggest obstacle to our taking this Step is that we are afraid to face the unpleasant aspects of our past, especially where we have been at fault.

The first part of the Eighth Step is neither difficult to understand nor hard to go through with. As a matter of fact, if we have written out our Fourth Step inventory, we may already have the list of persons we have harmed. However, becoming willing to make amends to them all is another matter. To make amends means to mend or repair, in this case damaged relationships with people, organizations and institutions we have wronged.

This Eighth Step is to our relations with others what the Fourth was to our relations with ourselves. And obviously the Ninth and Fifth Steps are similarly related to one another. When I went through with the Fourth Step inventory for the first time, it was with the understanding that I would move on to the Fifth Step as soon as possible. Clearly, I do well to approach this "became willing" part of the Eighth Step with the idea that it feeds directly into the action in Step Nine of going out and making such amends as I can.

Here honesty becomes all important. The quickest way for me to put myself in bad relationship with the Step is to kid myself that I am willing to make an amend if I am not really completely ready. The best method I know of for dealing with unwillingness is this: 1) face it honestly, 2) remember that I have agreed to "go to any lengths to gain victory over alcohol," and 3) ask God to make me willing. This approach works—maybe not in five minutes—but if persisted in, it does work.

Then the question arises of just what constitutes an amend. Many of us find that the old rationalization, "If I stay sober, that's amends enough to those I have hurt," just doesn't work. We have to be willing to go further. Some of the most common amends have to do with: people we owe money; wives, parents, children, relatives and friends we have mistreated; employers, employees and business associates we have harmed; people with whom we have become involved morally in an injurious manner.

This list is only a partial one, but it gives a pretty good general idea of the different types of messes we are dealing with. It is impossible to lay down general rules for handling these various situations. For me, there is no substitute for sitting down with my sponsor and thrashing out each individual case, keeping in mind the intention to do whatever turns out to be necessary to thoroughly and honestly go through with the Step.

In the case of money amends, I didn't have enough money to make them all good at once, but a willingness to pay when and as I could, backed up by small monthly installments, did wonders in putting matters right. In the case of family members I had wronged, a sincere apology was often amend enough, although I sometimes found it difficult to become willing to go even this far.

My natural inclination with unpleasant life situations or soured personal relationships is to sweep them under the rug, look the other way, justify myself and hope they will resolve themselves in time. It seems to be a plausible enough approach but, unfortunately, it never worked very well. These wrongs refused to stay forgotten, didn't resolve themselves, and even thrived on this treatment to the extent that they drove me back to the first drink again and again.

Facing the people I had hurt and the difficulties I had created seemed impossible, but those who had gone before me on the road to recovery in AA assured me that not only was this method possible but, if followed through, it produced freedom from the guilt, fear, self-pity, resentment and depression which these situations had produced in my life.

I gained faith in the principle which the Eighth Step is about, through experience. When I went through with the process, it did produce the results my sponsor and AA friends said it would.

I'm a guy who used to make "God" out of what others thought of me. This Step helped free me from a slavish dependence on other people's opinions. It helped teach me the value of placing principles before personalities in my life. It is not a Step that I feel I have taken. What I have made is a beginning. As it says in Chapter Five of the Big Book, "We are not saints." I still have character defects, and I still hurt other people (though not as often or seriously as before AA). Each time I become aware of an amend I owe, there is another chance to become willing with God's help to put the principles of the AA program before my fear of personalities (mine or anyone else's).

The wonderful thing about growth in the program is that each time I make a right decision in the area of becoming willing to make an amend it makes the next one a little easier to make. And strangely, I find that the more willing I become to admit it when I am wrong, the less often am I in the position of having to make such an admission. Sure I am still wrong, but only sometimes now—not all the time as I used to be.

T.P., Jr.

Persons We Had Harmed

September 1979

In mental preparation of my Eighth Step list, I discovered that some names came to mind naturally. In most instances, we want to change for the better where our children and family are concerned.

However, I found there were other people I did not want to make amends to, people I held some resentments toward—so I impulsively concluded they didn't deserve any amends. I have to keep in mind that had I behaved in a more reasonable manner, they might not have responded as they did. If the circumstances had been reversed, I might have taken the same action they chose. I have to allow others to make mistakes and be human. Harboring resentments because of something others did is, in effect, imposing my values upon them. By imposing my standards upon them, I am trying to assume God's role. I must realize I am not responsible for the actions of others, whether I approve of them or not. If I take on that task, I am passing judgment on them for reacting in a way that was unacceptable to me. I am taking their inventory.

In this Step, it states that we "became willing to make amends." This implies that there is going to be some conscious effort on my part to make all the needed amends. Those that come easy, to my old way of reasoning, would be an excellent stopping point. Yet the Step says we became willing to make amends to all those we had harmed. In going to these other people, I don't need to crawl or go on and on about how sorry I am, because this would make me appear worthless. I don't believe I need apologize for being human; rather, I simply need to acknowledge that I was at fault and humbly ask them to pardon me. I do not need to make amends on my hands and knees; I need to walk tall, without false pride. When I go in humility and sincerely ask people to forgive me, this will remove the burden from my shoulders. They, too, may have been at fault, but I am neither their God nor their conscience. I am responsible only for myself.

For me, this Step offers two features: I am being responsible, by owning up to my wrongs and making amends for them; at the same time, I accept others as they are, regardless of what they did, or of what they may do when I go to them to make amends.

It's a Step with a double feature. When doing it, we make a double play. After finishing it, we receive double indemnity. Our reward is two for the price of one.

B.D.
Reynoldsburg, Ohio

The Eighth Step

October 1977

Around the tables, I have, of late, participated in a succession of discussions centering on the Eighth Step. I regard this Step as the easiest but perhaps the most subtle in the program. It requires only that I make a list of people I have harmed and become willing to make amends to them all. Unlike Step Five, Eight does not require that I seek out a companion and unload it on him. It does not require searching my soul or being humble—only making a list and becoming willing. Step Nine requires some damn bold action, so it is very different from, though obviously dependent on, Step Eight.

The Eighth Step relates to people other than me. Unquestionably, it points outward and not inward. Many of us feel anger about this position and protest, "I didn't hurt anyone else but me. I figure I have to make amends to me." The phrasing may vary, but the idea is always the same: "Make amends to me." Frankly, I think this is so much garbage. It's one of the "old ideas" the Big Book advises us to discard—namely, selfishness. If the founders had meant Eight and Nine to be directed at themselves, they would have so stated in plain English.

But here's an AA paradox: I have found, to my great joy, that if I work on Eight and Nine and keep the emphasis on my relationships with others, these Steps actually do bring about the ultimate amends to me—a happy, sober day-to-day life that brims over with gladness, happiness, good fortune and all that I could wish for. It's far better to work on the Steps the way the Big Book and the "Twelve and Twelve" suggest than to risk losing this great life.

Anonymous

Ham on Wry

January 1990

Rich M. of Milwaukee, Wisconsin swears that in "Shoplifters Anonymous," the last part of their Eighth Step reads: "... became willing to make amends to the mall."

Thinking It Through

August 2001

I had just married and moved from Canada to Barbados and was beginning to feel settled, even comfortable, in my new surroundings and my new AA group. After a few months, I decided it was time to take the plunge, make the list, and complete my Eighth Step. "Half measures availed us nothing" seemed louder than ever at meetings, and inaction on the Steps, I believe, is a dangerous thing for me.

So convinced, I read the Big Book, the "Twelve and Twelve," and talked with my sponsor.

It's just a list, I figured, that's all. I had no idea how limiting my thinking was. Just beginning this Step has had a profound impact on my life. So far, there are sixty or so people on my list, and I'm not finished.

I don't know how this life change has happened, but since beginning the Eighth Step I have stopped buying into my excuses. For example, rather than be miserable and blame everything on some person, place or thing, I look at myself first. Rather than blow up at a person, I call my sponsor. Rather than judge someone who is angry toward me, I think, How would I like to be treated here?—and actually apply it. Sometimes I don't feel I know the person in my head anymore. I like this new one better.

Recently, I was upset with my husband and decided to call him at his office to tell him precisely what was wrong with him (thank goodness he has Al-Anon). I sat down at the phone, picked it up—and called my sponsor instead. We talked about why I was upset and about recovery. At the end of the conversation, I told her that I wasn't going to call my husband but would instead read *Dr. Bob and the Good Oldtimers*. And I actually did! This is not the me I know.

Lying on the couch with the book, I felt a mix of feelings. The book describes what Dr. Bob and Bill used to read regularly at meetings or to other drunks before the Big Book came along: the Sermon on the Mount, the Book of James, and First Corinthians, thirteenth chapter. I am not a Bible reader, but I figured it certainly couldn't hurt, and it was something to take my mind off my perceived problems. I grabbed the Bible and read. There it was, the injunction to "turn the other cheek." Right then, reading those words, something happened.

Maybe my husband was inconsiderate. Maybe he did do something to upset me. Who knows, and who cares? I thought. What about my behavior? I started looking at myself and I was not pleased at what I saw. I sat there with the book on my lap and thought about my actions, my words, my behavior, my crazy feelings. I turned the camera on myself rather than on my husband. Next came this thought: What if, regardless of how others acted, I treated them well so that my actions were good and kind and necessary and true? What if I responded with "Is something upsetting you?" rather than "Stop talking to me like that, you (insert judgmental comment here)"? What if I were caring rather than judgmental?

When my husband came home, he expected me to be angry. If my past actions were any indication, he had every right to this expectation. He tried to avoid me and dismissed my attempt at casual conversation. Our meeting did not begin well, and yes, my buttons were pushed. However, my Eighth Step list, the Big Book, and *Dr. Bob and the Good Oldtimers* were on the table in front of me and made me stop. How would he like to be treated?, I asked myself, and no anger came. My husband and I ended up talking like civil human beings, and it was wonderful.

I see the change in many areas of my life. I'm less likely to react. I do this for partly selfish reasons, too: I don't want to add any more names to my list. Sometimes this is plain old work. I am forced to think of a better, healthier, non-amends-requiring action. I pray and think it through. In several cases, thankfully, the emotions—be they sad, angry or indifferent—left me before the answer arrived so I was able to go forward through difficult situations without my emotions in the way, having a clear head and a clear conscience.

When on the verge of reacting, I often think about what my friend Katherine once said to me about dogs and cats and the messes they create. "It's odd," she said, "how when an animal does something wrong, we simply let it know it has misbehaved, and then we promptly forget about it." I have never found myself mad at an animal for an hour, let alone weeks, months, or years. This helps me to balance situations I find myself in.

If these are the results of the Eighth Step, I can hardly wait to see the promises the Ninth Step holds.

Brenda B.
Barbados

STEP NINE

"Made direct amends to such people wherever possible, except when to do so would injure them or others."

Our real purpose is to fit ourselves to be of maximum service to God and the people about us," reads the Big Book.

We are putting our lives in order with the Ninth Step. It is just after completion of this Step, actually, when the Promises appear in the Big Book: "We will suddenly realize that God is doing for us what we could not do for ourselves."

Making amends is not easy, as the Grapevine stories in this section will show. One writer felt she needed to take responsibility and make amends for her part in an abusive relationship. Another AA was able to make amends to his violent, alcoholic father long after the father had died. A third admits to stealing a wallet from a favorite uncle.

None of these amends came simply, but with consultation with sponsors and other AAs, prayer, and guidance from a Higher Power.

A member who had embezzled a large amount of money from an employer writes in a 2006 Grapevine story that his sponsor advises him to turn himself in and make amends; he initially says no.

"I knew that I really had no choice. I wanted the Promises that are promised to each of us. I needed this lifted from my shoulders, or I would drink again." Because of this amends he spends 18 months in jail, but he realizes, "When I am released, I will be six years sober, a free man with no baggage or secrets."

Scary as this process is, it is vital in our recovery from alcoholism. "We are willing. We have to be," the Big Book says. "We must not shrink at anything."

Rewards of Step Nine

April 1979 (PO Box 1980)

At the end of my amends list was the name of a city editor whom I had worked for during my drinking days. I knew he held me in low regard because of my past performance as a reporter. The thought of making direct amends to him overwhelmed me. Besides, I reasoned, it might ruin my reputation and professional credibility.

But after being sober five years, I found that the man's name still haunted me. Somehow, I knew that I must face him in person. By coincidence, an AA state convention was to be held in a city near where I formerly worked. So I considered stopping there to see if the man was still city editor.

On the day of the convention, I prayed constantly for courage to go through with my mission. I phoned him, and he agreed to meet me at his office. Going back to that newspaper office was one of the hardest tasks in my life. When I met him, he didn't look angry. In fact, we engaged in small talk for several minutes. Then, I explained why I was there.

I told him about the Fellowship and the importance of thoroughly taking the Steps to the best of one's ability. He was very compassionate and understanding. When I left, a deep guilt had been lifted from me, and I felt whole. All the way back home, I thanked God again and again for Step Nine.

R.P.
Seaside, Oregon

The Amends I Most Dreaded to Make

August 1977

I had made all my amends but one. I had faced my father, my mother, my brothers, my second ex-wife, and numerous employers and acquaintances I had stolen from or cheated. The results had been incredible. Every one of them was kind and appreciative of what I was trying to do with my life. Many of them told me, "If there's anything I can do for you, please let me know." The peace I was beginning to experience was astounding. I also kept a list of the people I wasn't able to locate, in case I should ever come into contact with them.

Now, there was no more rationalizing, no more amends to make in order to delay the one I dreaded most.

She was a pedestrian I ran down in September of 1965. She was rushed to the hospital with a brain hemorrhage and wasn't expected to live. There were investigators looking for me, and I kept avoiding them. When I was sent back to jail for the sixth and last time, I learned that she had been released from the hospital at her request and was returning to her home in Brussels, Belgium. That was all I knew. I had no idea what condition she was in. I didn't want to know. I was paying the price for my mistake in time behind bars. My debt was paid.

I had my last drink two years after the accident. I had just spent eight months trying to stay sober without those damn Steps, and the results had been nil. This time, I decided to give them a try. I had some difficulty understanding and coming to terms with some of the Steps in the beginning. I guess we all do. But eventually, the understanding came and the application followed.

Now, without realizing how far I'd come, I knew I had to face up to the one amends I had dreaded ever since I had come to comprehend Step Nine. That little voice inside me wouldn't let up. I had to do it.

I really didn't know where to start, where to find her. I looked at the police report, found her address in Belgium, and wrote to her. The letter was returned: "Addressee Unknown." I called the Belgian consulate in Los Angeles. They told me there was nothing they could do, but that I might write the American embassy in Brussels. I did.

Then the news: "In response to your letter of April 27, 1972, I regret to inform you that Miss W____ died in Belgium in 1966 shortly after her return from the United States. This information was provided to the embassy by her last known employer."

Oh my God, no! Not because of the accident. How would I know for sure? I was torn. Part of me was saying I had done all I could do and I would have to learn to accept it. But another part of me felt uneasy and unsettled. Then I realized that she must have had a family, and that I certainly owed them amends.

In her medical jacket at the hospital, I found the addresses of a sister in Canada and two doctors in Belgium. I wrote my letter of amends to the sister. It, too, came back: "Addressee Unknown." I wrote to both doctors in Belgium. Six months later, I received a reply from one of them. He commended what I was trying to do and sent the sister's address, in Belgium. I wrote my letter of amends again. In two weeks, I had a reply in Flemish. It took another week to have it translated.

> This morning, we received your letter. I thank you with all my heart. Perhaps your letter helped to cure the deep wound that was caused by the death of my only, loved, younger sister. Yes, she is dead following that

accident. It was terribly hard. It still causes such a strong pain. We loved each other enormously. She was an artist; later, I shall send you a copy of one of her works.

The Insurance concerning the accident was paid to us [the writer and her husband], the trip and the burial by us. We suffered financially terribly much because of her death. She helped us very much. She was a good person. She was so dear to me. A day does not go by without my thinking about her. We have one child, Julie, eight years old. I am sending a picture taken on the day of her first communion.

We are not rich, but my husband and I are very happy together, and are taking care of everything together with love. We do not want to profit by you. You must pay nothing. If you want, and if you can, perhaps give something to put in Julie's savings account. She will remain alone in life sometimes. But you must not defraud yourself of anything. I would be completely glad about that—the money for the child. I am a schoolteacher, and I try to make a good person out of my child.

I keep your letter for Julie. And will you write a small letter off and on? That also I would like very much. And you must pray for us and all those who have lost someone in an accident. It is so hard. Life is so short. I am so glad, so very glad that you have written. I am so thankful to you. I shall finish for now, for I must go to school. Julie also prays for you and sends her best regards. I hope you find someone who will translate the letter to you, because I don't know enough English. God is good and merciful, and we must be like that also. God bless you.

I did write again. The letters I received have been even warmer. I found it hard to believe and accept. How could anyone have that much love and forgiveness? Like most of my life in AA, it was too much to comprehend. Then we began to correspond about seeing each other someday and how nice it would be to sit and talk face-to-face.

In July 1974, I flew to New York to meet my nine-year-old daughter, who was going with me to Belgium. This was at the suggestion of my ex-wife, and I was startled by her new trust in me. I was impressed that I had changed that much.

It was difficult for my daughter, leaving her mother for the first time. I hadn't seen her in three years, and never had it been just the two of us. On the plane, we had dinner and went to sleep. I woke up suddenly, just before we began our descent into Brussels, and she was standing over me, just looking at me. Then she was in my arms crying, and I felt for the first time in my life the overwhelming and beautiful responsibility of being a parent.

I don't have the words to describe our trip to Belgium. When we were met at the airport by our Belgian friends, we embraced and cried as if we had known one another for years. We lived in their home for two weeks. Our daughters were instant friends in spite of the language barrier. My daughter and I were given a grand tour of western Belgium. We crossed the English Channel from France to Dover. Everything was done for us. They fed us, washed our clothes, and introduced us to their friends. And when the girls had gone to bed, we spent many hours talking about the accident and its aftermath, talking and crying together. My daughter and I were loved in a way so total and so foreign to me that I thought there must be a catch. It scared the hell out of me. One day, they told me that if anything happened to them, I would have to come to Belgium and take care of everything. I was very flattered but had no concept of the depth of what they were saying until my final day there.

At five o'clock on the morning we were to leave Belgium, I awoke to find sitting at the foot of my bed the sister of the woman I killed in 1965. She was crying and looking at me intently. Then, very softly, she said, "You are my brother. My real brother. My very dear and real brother. Don't ever forget that."

I never have. I doubt that I ever will.

D.S.

Desert Hot Springs, California

Right to the Edge

April 2006

My name is Ross R., and I am forty-one years old. I am currently serving an eighteen-month sentence in a federal prison, a sentence that resulted from making my Ninth Step amends.

I came to AA on February 28, 1999, and have been sober ever since. A thorough Ninth Step and willingness to do anything my sponsor asked has helped me remain sober.

On January 2, 2000, when I was eleven months sober, my sponsor, Olaf G., and I went hiking in the Hollywood Hills. We discussed my Ninth Step; I knew he would bring up the one amend I had not made. For seven years, I had embezzled quite a large amount of money from an employer. I quit that job in my third month of sobriety because I could not stop stealing. My sponsor told me that he had discussed my situation with many old-timers and had been directed to the Big Book for the answer.

I had no family to support, my sponsor said, and following his direction would not harm others. He advised me to turn myself in to that company and make amends.

I wish I could say I followed his directions without question right away, but I told him no. He gave me two weeks to decide. In the meantime, he asked that I read the Big Book and pray. I said I would.

I took the two weeks, but I knew that I really had no choice. I wanted the Promises that are promised to each of us. I needed this lifted from my shoulders, or I would drink again.

On January 12, 2000, I went to my former employer and made my amends. What started out as one of my worst days—because I was so scared—became one of my best days when it was over. Because I had trusted God, my sponsor, and AA, that trinity had lifted the weight that was on my shoulders for so long. I felt sober.

What I thought would be a quick process turned into three and a half years of waiting. In March 2003, federal government representatives came to my apartment and presented me with a plea agreement that would place me in prison for anywhere from eighteen months to five years.

Once again, I fell back in the arms of AA. Fortunately, I had kept going to meetings and had a sponsor, so I had a support network helping me during that time. I found a lawyer in the program; she walked me through this process with incredible dignity and grace. I started sharing at any meeting I could, trying to find people with an experience similar to this. I would be lying if I said I didn't go through many days resenting the amends and feeling alone in my process. My sponsor and support group helped me realize that I am not alone, and my experience would one day help someone else.

The day of sentencing came. I cannot describe how overwhelming that is to experience. Your future held in the hands of others, and an overwhelming regret that past behavior has brought you to this point. I shared these feelings at meetings. On sentencing day, AA packed the courthouse with over seventy fellow AAs showing their support. That awful day turned into one of great meaning and we felt a spiritual experience in that courtroom.

The judge said she had never seen such a large turnout for anyone in all her years on the bench. Prosecutors recommended the minimum sentence and I was sentenced to eighteen months in federal prison.

My sponsor and an AA buddy took me in to surrender on the day ordered and will be there to pick me up on the day I get out, as long as we all stay sober.

I spent the first eight days in a maximum-security prison and I can say they were the worst days of my life. I was angry with God and with AA, and felt abandoned by both. On the seventh day, I got on my knees and prayed to God, saying that I had enough and could not go on anymore. They moved me the next morning to where I am today and, once again, I was reminded that God never gives me more than I can handle, but sometimes he takes me right to the edge.

When I am released, I will be six years sober, a free man with no baggage or secrets. AA will be there for me, and I will be there for it. If I can spend the rest of my life helping others in the walk of sobriety, then I will have a good life.

Ross R.

Taft, California

A Pat on the Back

September 2001

When I was just shy of my fifth AA birthday, I finally completed my Eighth Step, and I was very proud of the list I had compiled of the people I'd harmed and was willing to make amends to. I even carried a pocket notebook around with me so that as names from the past popped into mind I could jot them down. The list had dozens of names on it, and several "John Does" whose names I couldn't remember.

But as I looked over the list, I realized it was missing the name of one of the most important people in my life: my mother's. Why had I forgotten hers? Her name was left off because I didn't think I could make direct amends to her since she was in a hospital suffering from Alzheimer's disease, and it had been several years since she had recognized or talked to anybody. Since she wouldn't know who I was, I saw no use in trying to make amends to her.

Nothing I read in AA literature, however, told me that I could make amends only to people who could talk to me. In fact, the Ninth Step said I was to make "direct amends ... whenever possible," and there was no valid reason why I couldn't make amends to my mother.

Although my mother didn't react to people, she was physically active and spent hours walking around the yard of the nursing home. She would walk in a straight line, with her hands held to her chest, until she met a fence or a tree and then she would make a sharp turn and continue on until she met another obstacle.

During a visit to the nursing home, I joined her, putting my arm around her and walking with her as I made my amends. I told her that I was her youngest son, that I loved her and missed her, and that I was an alcoholic and had done many things I knew had hurt her.

I was crying by this time, but as we walked together I continued. I told her that I was sober and met with other alcoholics who helped me stay sober, and that one of the things I had to do was make amends to people I had harmed. And I told her I had to do more than just apologize to her for the harm I had done; I had to make changes. There was no reaction from my mother as we walked, but patients and staff certainly had odd looks for the crying, middle-aged man walking with his arm around a five-foot-tall woman who hadn't spoken to anyone for three years.

My mother was not reacting at all to what I had to say, but I continued with my amends. I would, I told her, try to make amends to her in two ways. First, I would continue to do what I had done for over four years to stay sober: go to meetings, pray, read the Big Book, and work with other alcoholics ... and do it just a day at a time. Second, every day I would try to do something nice for somebody, without telling anyone what I had done. If I did tell someone about my good deed, then that deed wouldn't count as part of my amends. Maybe I would empty an ashtray or pick up a piece of litter or slow down on the freeway so a car could get into my lane. Whatever I did, it was to be spontaneous and dedicated to my mother.

As I finished telling my mother all of this, I felt something touch my back. I had been talking and crying and not paying much attention to anything except keeping pace with my mother and telling her my story, and I assumed someone was walking behind us without me knowing it. But when I turned around, no one was there. What I had felt was my mother's hand as she put her arm around my back and patted me.

Did she understand what I'd told her? I don't know. She never patted me again, or reacted to me or other visitors. I chose to believe, however, that through my mother my Higher Power had told me that I'd done the right thing, and that, as a gift, I was being left not with the memory of a mother who had lost contact with the world, but with the memory of a mother who could still show her love and forgiveness.

That was a gift I never would have received if I was still on the streets drinking.

Dale C.
Tacoma, Washington

Scene of the Crime

September 1993

The rocks looked the same. The light in the sky at sunset was as I remembered it; the stillness and silence of the pinyon-juniper forest had not changed. This was the day I returned to the windswept landscape of northern Arizona from which I had fled five years before.
When I left, I was running from my alcoholism. I went 4,000 miles north of this

land of open skies and silence, only to find that my disease came the distance with me. Once into recovery, I stayed where I had landed, building a foundation through the Twelve Steps of Alcoholics Anonymous for a life of sobriety and serenity.

But I knew, during the years I stayed in Alaska, that I would one day return to the scene of my crimes, for I had an amends to make there. So I found myself, during a vacation in the Southwest, driving the familiar road toward my old home. The time had finally come to face a ghost from the past.

In Sedona, I passed that same laundromat where the violence had first erupted, back in 1981. I should have left him then, but I didn't. There were a million reasons for me to stay, but the most important was that he was my drinking buddy, my provider. We drank and battled and made up for three more stormy years after the laundromat scene. I had been too fearful to leave him, too addicted to turn my back. The heart-pounding fear of his violent nature came back to me as I drove through town. I found the nearest meeting.

Appropriately, the topic of the meeting was fear. When I was called on, I told the group that I was going to make amends to a man I feared; I confessed it was possible that he might hit me again, or worse. Although five years had passed since I had escaped from him, I was not at all convinced that he would greet me warmly. Nevertheless, the amends had to be made. Step Nine said that I had to admit to him where I was wrong. I chose to do this face to face.

A man sitting across the table from me spoke next. "Fear keeps a lot of us from making amends," he said. "But I have found no other way to resolve those conflicts which arise from the harm we do to others. You can face the man with courage."

He smiled at me. "Courage is fear that has said its prayers."

In Flagstaff the next morning, I sat in a restaurant where I had sat a hundred times before, drinking coffee with shaky hands. The ghosts were moving and talking to me from the walls, and the fearful part of me wanted to run away again. I prayed for courage and went on.

Closer still to my old stomping grounds, I stopped the car along the highway, deciding to walk a couple of miles to reach a volcano crater. I hiked along, lost in my own thoughts, hearing voices from the past. Once over the lava wall, I entered the volcano crater quietly. An eerie wind blew, creating jet stream highways for the birds and sweeping the air clean. The sun passed behind a tall spire of rock at noon and a shadow fell across my lap.

The volcano crater was a place of stillness and meditation. Five years before, I had come to this same place to make the decision to leave the Southwest for Alaska. I had felt at once terrified and aroused by the prospect of a major change. On that fateful day, lacking the perspective of distance and sobriety, I had taken a long look at my life and made a guess about the best path to take. I remembered these things now, as I admired the silhouette of a big old ponderosa pine against the curve of volcanic basalt. And I asked again for the courage to go back to face the man I had hurt by my choice of paths.

Later that afternoon, I cruised slowly through the neighborhood in which he and I had once lived. I looked at each little wood house for a clue as to which was his. Part of me secretly hoped he would no longer be there.

When I saw it, I drove past, backed up, pulled into the driveway, and then very nearly pulled back out. His car was there. Children's toys littered the yard. His name was on a sign next to the door.

Maybe he's at work, I thought, panicking. Maybe his wife doesn't want me around. My feet walked toward the door of their own accord. My heart was pounding. My face stung as though he had already slapped me.

When he came to the door, he recognized me immediately. With only a slight hesitation, he invited me in, introduced me to his children, and offered me a chair. Visibly nervous, I told him I couldn't stay long, but that I had some things to say.

He went to get a beer, offered me one. I suddenly wondered what I was doing there. His home was a slippery place. Sending up another quick prayer for my Higher Power to put the right words in my mouth, I began to speak.

"I've come to tell you what happened when I left you," I said. "I told you I'd come back. I was lying to you when I made that promise, because I knew in my heart that I was never going to return. My disappearance hurt you, and I apologize for that."

He began to protest, to rewrite that five-year-old piece of history, to tell me how it happened. I had to interrupt him and ask him to let me have my say; for a moment, it felt like old times, me arguing with him about the facts.

"I am sober now," I told him, "and it's important for me to come back here and tell you that the problems we had in our relationship were at least fifty percent my fault. I always blamed you for everything—for my alcoholism, for my failures, for my misery. Those things were not your fault. You were good to me in many ways."

He didn't know how to answer me. So instead he drank some more beer and asked about my family. As I sat in that man's living room I watched his stature diminish before my eyes. No longer was he a cruel and vengeful lunatic. No longer did he possess the power to terrify me. He was just a man with an alcohol problem. The moment I saw him for what he was, I could forgive him, for his problem was no different than mine. He just hadn't found a solution yet. He wasn't looking for a solution yet. I asked my Higher Power to be with him, and all the anger and fear dissolved into pity for a man still battered by his disease.

Soon I got up and prepared to leave. I thanked him for taking the time to listen to what I had to say. Shyly, he stuck out his hand toward me. I grasped it, then impulsively stepped forward and hugged him.

I drove away from the house without looking back. My shoulders felt light, as if a giant weight had been lifted. Until it was lifted, I hadn't even been aware it was there.

The tortured autopsies I had performed on that relationship were finally behind me. For the first time, I was able to let him go. He did not hit me. He did not seduce me. His power over me was broken at last.

I enjoyed a buoyancy of spirit after that visit. By admitting where I was at fault, I was given the ability to forgive a man who had held me in bondage for years after I had left him. With forgiveness came a freedom that I had not anticipated. The amends had required nothing but courage, and a faith that my Higher Power would carry me where I had been too afraid to walk alone.

Kit K.
Sterling

I Stole the Wallet

August 2010

When I was growing up I had a favorite uncle whom I've come to believe was an alcoholic, just like me. I was always excited to be around this uncle. He drank and seemed to have a lot of fun. At one time, he was a deputy sheriff, and so he knew everyone from one end of the county to the other. The first time I drank was with him, and the first time I got really drunk was with him—at the ripe old age of 11.

I was 18 years old when I was drunk one Sunday night and broke, so I drove up to his place to see if I could borrow some money. I found both him and a man who was living with him passed out. I stole the wallet of the man living with him and left the house unnoticed.

This man blamed my uncle for stealing his money. The sheriff was called in. My uncle had worked for him and had drunk himself out of that job. It was very embarrassing and shameful for my uncle to go through that. Eventually, it blew over.

I left for the Marine Corps and tried to forget about the incident, but every now and then when I was back home I would think about it when I ran into my uncle. I felt a lot of guilt and shame when it came up in my thoughts, and I drank to make it go away. It was like a monkey on my back.

When I sobered up and was in treatment, this came up in my Fourth and Fifth Steps, so obviously it was on my Eighth Step list. It was meant to clear up the wreckage of my past so I didn't have to have it haunt me for the rest of my life.

My uncle, although a fun-loving man, had a very volatile temper. I was scared, to say the least, but I knew I had to make that amends. I met with him on a Saturday morning in his garage and brought up the incident. He remembered it as though it were yesterday. I told him that I was the one who stole the money. Believe me, I was extremely uncomfortable. It was very awkward for both of us. I was, you could say, the apple of his eye and we had done many things together, so it really took him for a loop. I asked my uncle for forgiveness and told him I was very sorry for the misery I had caused him.

He looked me right in the eye and said, "Lee, what's between us is between us, and that's the end of it." When I walked out of that garage I was a free man, released of the bondage of self. This gave me faith that I was on the right path and that this AA business worked.

Years later this same uncle was in an assisted care home. He needed help with his affairs but was strongly rejecting help, even from a very close brother, another uncle of mine. This other uncle asked me to help him. I met with my first uncle and told him we loved him and wanted to help him, but we needed his help to go through a power of attorney hearing. With much skepticism on the part of a court administrator and others, the next day we had the proceeding. I prayed for the strength to go through with this and was prepared for the worst, but everything went without a hitch and people walked out of the room shaking their heads. I put my arms around my uncle and just cried. I know that when I made that amends to him years before he knew I wouldn't lie to him and he trusted me to do the right thing. Six months later he passed away and my other uncle was able to handle the estate without any glitches. There's only one way this would have happened and that is with God's help and guidance.

Lee C.J.
Fargo, North Dakota

Heard at Meetings

February 2009

I had a really good reason for working Step Nine and making amends to my family and friends: I didn't want a parade of people at my funeral singing, "Ding, dong, the wicked witch is dead!"

Carol K.
Sarasota, Florida

STEP TEN

"Continued to take personal inventory and when we were wrong promptly admitted it."

Step Ten is not an overnight matter, but rather continues for a lifetime. AAs take regular inventory and watch out for selfishness, dishonesty, resentment and fear. "We make amends quickly when they pop up," the Big Book says. But our goal is "progress, not perfection." The soul-searching required by this Step helps AAs correct what is wrong. This could happen in a spot-check inventory, a day's end balance sheet or a periodic review of progress, or perhaps an annual or semi-annual housecleaning.

Step Ten has helped AAs stay on track spiritually and helped prevent bad situations from becoming worse.

"Step Ten has saved me from more mistakes than I can count. But time and again, I've delayed taking this Step—because of pride and fear. One of my sneakiest evasions has simply been in posing as morally superior to the person I have wronged," an AA writes in a 1992 Grapevine story.

AAs, in the following stories, talk about emotional dry-benders, the need to practice restraint of tongue and pen, and the dangers of "justifiable" anger—which, the "Twelve and Twelve" says, "ought to be left with someone better qualified to handle it."

One popular theme running throughout these stories is the importance of focusing on ourselves. The Tenth Step says nothing about another person's wrongs, the author of the 1992 story points out. "The only issue I ever have to deal with is any wrong I have committed in thought or deed."

Like a Ship at Sea

October 1950

n search for a daily "operating schedule" which would help to make the Tenth Step habitual and as pleasant as possible, the writer hit upon the following analogy and found it helpful.

On a ship's bridge, at sea, the navigator is charged with keeping his ship on her course. When he is piloting near islands, shoals and coastal waters, he must constantly take sights or bearings of rocks, light-houses, mountain peaks and other reference points that appear on his chart. The compass bearings of these objects from his ship enable him to mark his progress on the chart and to steer a safe course.

The point of the analogy is that the navigator constantly regards each of the menacing objects in the sea around him as aids to the safe passage of his vessel. As long as he notes the bearing of each one it cannot harm him.

The "sighting" or experiencing of fear, resentment, self-pity, anger and self-righteousness doesn't mean that the ship is off her course at all. Each is a menace to be expected and encountered every day of a normal busy life. If, however, the watch on the bridge is habitually alert, the menace can be an aid to safe passage.

Frank M.
Piedmont, California

The Tenth Step

December 1975

n getting an apartment ready for a new tenant, who also happened to be an AA and a real friend of mine, I "salvaged" three full gallon cans of paint from the partially decorated confines of that apartment and hid them in my own place. My scheme was to sell the new tenant the three gallons to finish the badly needed painting, for a total of fifteen bucks.

After sleeping on that plot—or not sleeping, but tossing—I awoke early feeling upset about something that I couldn't figure out. Facing the uneasiness squarely, I began to search the Twelve Steps with a desire to understand the problem. After just one inventory of the previous day's dealings, I came up with the awareness that my old con tactics were recurring; I had tricked myself into thinking I could be comfortable with making a lousy fifteen dollars by cheating and lying to another AA member.

Now, being aware of what I had done, was I going to continue to let this bug me to distraction? Or should I use the honesty of the rest of the Tenth Step and ask for forgiveness? I decided that the best way was to approach my friend with what I had done and take the consequences. Whether they were good or bad, I would feel clean of the garbage.

I proceeded to ask my friend if I could take a Tenth Step. And I did. His answer was beautiful: "Thank you for being honest. We all have character defects, and they trigger us back to the old habits that drove us to drink, because we weren't measuring up to what we thought we should be." It was out! Thank God, it came from one who was able to forgive another human error.

That's what the Tenth Step did for me today. Without the promptness of the admission, I wouldn't have had only one sleepless night; it could have been nights upon end. This AA way of life has many rewards if we search for the honest way to live it. I'm very happy with the continuing rewards that I am aware of. If only we can see what is making our lives uncomfortable! Try the Tenth Step again, buddy. I'm glad I tried it today.

J.M.
Rantoul, Illinois

It Takes Practice to Be Human

December 1977

During my drinking days, it seemed that I was either a god or a devil—but never human. I was either so grandly above everyone else that they were unworthy of my love or so desperately below the level of everyone else that I felt myself unworthy of their affection. When I was in my deluded god state, I was perfect, all good and almighty. When I was in my depressed devil state, I was totally useless and worthless, hopelessly flawed.

After I stopped drinking and started to work the simple program that AA gave me, I gradually started to experience life in that condition between godhood and devilhood called humanity. Little by little, I came to learn that, while I wasn't as great as I sometimes fancied myself, neither was I as loathsome as I often felt. Passage of time and reworking of the Steps taught me that I was neither a god nor a devil but rather a human being. Eventually, I learned that a human being is neither wholly good nor completely bad, but that a human being has the capability of doing either good or bad (or both).

I now believe that it is my lot as a human being, during my brief life, to help and harm, give and take, create and destroy, for I am neither perfect nor wholly evil. I also believe that my life will be a good life rather than a bad one if, at its end, I can honestly say that I helped more than I harmed, gave more than I took, and created more than I destroyed.

AA has taught me that the only way to work toward that goal is to do it on a day-at-a-time basis. So each night, I think of the Tenth Step and ask myself, "Have I, this day, helped more than I've harmed? Given more than I've taken? Created more than I've destroyed?"

M.B.
Minneapolis, Minnesota

In the Heat of Anger
September 1983

In the beginning of my new life as a sober alcoholic in AA, I prided myself (every day) in telling people in the program how easy it was for me to be sober, how easy it was not to feel the desire to drink, and most important, how one could progress with relatively little effort by working the program. About eight months after I took my last drink, experience began proving to me that living sober was not as easy as existing drunk. On the way to a Sunday noon meeting in Greenwich Village, something happened to me that will remain with me for the rest of my life.

That summer in New York, the heat had been overwhelming. It made me very uncomfortable. Angers and anxieties set in. One Sunday, I decided to go to an early meeting in the Village and then perhaps to Central Park for a walk, to try to cool off and think a little bit. My sister (who was visiting from Pennsylvania) and I boarded the No. 10 bus to the Village.

There were fewer than eight people on the bus. Sitting in front by the driver was a big woman in a red dress and a wide-brimmed hat. She sat there talking very loudly to the driver. My first reaction was: That woman is looking for attention. As the bus went down Broadway, the woman kept talking, and the driver, seemingly patient, listened, and so did I. My anger and resentment toward the woman grew.

At 42nd and Seventh Avenue, the driver turned to her and explained: "When you get off the bus, make a left, walk to the corner, and make a right at the corner. Then walk one block down the street, and you're there." He was telling her how to get to the Port Authority Bus Terminal at Eighth Avenue and 41st.

The woman remained seated. She told the driver he was confusing her. "One minute, you tell me to turn left. The next, you tell me to turn right. That doesn't make any sense to me!" The driver explained patiently that as she stepped off the bus, she should turn left, then walk to the corner and turn right, walk one block down the street, and she would be at the bus terminal.

The woman sat. "I just don't understand what you mean," she said. My anger was too much for me. I tried not to let it get to me. It was almost eleven-thirty, and we were not halfway to the Village. I would be late.

The woman sat and refused to get off until the driver made himself clear to her satisfaction. I lost control. The part of me that I thought I had buried eight months earlier came to life. I yelled, "Listen, woman! Get off the bus, walk to that corner over there, make a right, walk a block down, and you're there. What's so difficult about that?"

"Easy, buddy," the driver said, turning toward me. "She's blind."

I was numb. The bus moved closer to the corner to make it easy for her to step down. As she got off the bus, she said to me, "Be kind, mister. He's watching you from up there." She pointed to the sky. "I hope you have a nice day."

I didn't. The remainder of the day was a total haze for me. The thought of that woman and her words ringing in my mind kept me in touch with part of me I had thought was buried and forgotten. On the way back home, my sister wanted to stop at Macy's. She noticed that something was bothering me, and she asked me if I was okay. But it wasn't until that evening, when the two of us went to a Step meeting, that I told her how I was feeling.

"Why don't you share it?" she said. The workshop that evening was on the Tenth Step: "Continued to take personal inventory and when we were wrong promptly admitted it." At discussion time, I raised my hand to share the experience on the bus.

I couldn't speak. Tears filled my eyes. The leader let me pass. Toward the end of the meeting, I did manage to share my experience with my fellow alcoholics, and the load was lifted off my back.

Yes, living sober is difficult. But as painful as it might be, the learning through listening, the sharing, and the fellowship are worth more than I could ever have hoped for at the start of those first eight months.

I still find a lot of meaning in these words: "We can't bury the tyranny by killing the tyrant."

M.O.

Manhattan, New York

The Peace Process

December 1996 (PO Box 1980)

When I was drinking, I thought I was the most patient and tolerant person in the world. And I was—as long as things went my way. Today, after nearly twenty years in AA, I know that my impatience and intolerance are symptoms of my self-will. The question is how not to get trapped in the compelling pull of anger-based impatience and intolerance.

The Tenth Step offers immediate release from the bondage of self. Merely wanting to be patient and tolerant isn't enough. I have to develop the skill of the Tenth Step.

For me, asking God to remove the ill-feeling works pretty well. But if my anger persists, I need to do more. A quick, written inventory, using the approach taught in the Big Book, allows me to focus on the problem: me. Many times, I discover that the problem is mine, not the other person's. At this point, I'm often cleared of the angry feeling. But unless I do more, there's a strong chance it will return. What then?

Step Ten instructs me to share my self-investigation with another alcoholic—immediately. This prevents me from rationalizing the problem and talking myself out of the next part of the Step—the amends.

I have found that this angry feeling persists until I make amends. Then and only then am I free. Once the entire Tenth Step process is completed, I am at peace—and guess what? I'm very patient and tolerant.

Some people wonder what the presence of God feels like. I believe the peace I get from an effective Tenth Step is what God feels like.

Bruce T.
Gold River, California

Wrong Turn

October 1999

The first question I had about Step Ten was: How soon do I have to admit when I am wrong? "Promptly" seemed so vague. The answer from an AA old-timer was: "How long you been sober?" Annoyed, I asked back: "What has that got to do with it?" The answer was: "The longer you are sober, the shorter the 'promptly' gets!"

The next thing I had to learn about Step Ten is that it doesn't say anything about being "sorry." When I was drinking I had a constant stream of "Sorrys." Now that I have been free of the booze for a few thousand days, I rarely have to say I'm sorry, but I often have to say that I was wrong. There is a big difference.

I've been taught that if I say "I'm sorry" and then leave it like that, it means that I am leaving a lot unsaid that should be said. I am really asking for forgiveness or some sort of "general absolution." But that's not what this alcoholic usually needs.

What I need to say is how I was wrong and where I went wrong (thinking of the exact nature of my wrongs, Step Five). And, thinking of Step Nine, how am I going to make it up to the person or set things right? What are my amends here? No empty promises of "I'll never do it again!" No begging for forgiveness. An amends makes me work to put things back to the way they were before my wrong was committed.

To say I was wrong is also part of that AA medicine of ego deflation at depth. I'm not sorry because you are hurt but rather I am admitting that I am wrong because I did something to harm you. Big difference in my book!

I have spent time figuring out what exactly I was wrong about, and I have spent time figuring out a proposal of how I am going to straighten things out, since that too is my responsibility and not yours. But I am going to confer with you about this and not impose my solution on you. I may offer several options for you to choose from. I am going to continue a radically honest (but calm and tactful) dialogue with you in whatever way is appropriate.

Another thing I had to learn about this Step was that it means that I only take responsibility for when I was actually wrong. If I wasn't wrong on one part but was wrong on another, I say so. I cop it sweet for the parts that I was wrong about but not for the rest of it.

For instance, I often have to say something like: "Son, I want to tell you that I was way out of line by raising my voice and yelling at you like that. It was wrong of me to do it in a public place and in front of your friends because that is not only embarrassing but also rude and insensitive. In the future I propose to take you aside or wait until we are away from your mates. I will work on getting my volume and impulsive anger under control. Can you help me by telling me that I am yelling or that I am embarrassing you if I forget? On the other hand, I believe that what I said was correct. What you were doing was risky and a bit dangerous. I stand by my statement but was wrong to yell and embarrass you. I'll make it up to you by ...."

Lastly, I've been taught that this Step contains the most important word out of the 200 (count 'em) words in all of the Steps. That word is "continued." Makes a nice word to meditate upon.

Chuck F.
Canberra, Australia

Daily Reminder

December 2006 (PO Box 1980)

Without the habit of daily self-examination, I became overwhelmed by thoughts and feelings and made decisions out of fear. Eventually, I compromised my sobriety and relapsed.

In prison, I'm finding the need for a daily Tenth Step very important. Each day, when I wake up, I am reminded where my unchecked defects have brought me. But seeing my defects is not enough to make them improve or go away—the solution seems to be following awareness with action. God seems to want my daily cooperation.

I don't think the lack of a daily Tenth Step was the only reason I relapsed. But I can no longer afford to believe that the other eleven Steps will do my Tenth Step for me. I need to work all the Steps, just as the Big Book suggests.

David R.
Coldwater, Michigan

Safety Valve

October 2010

One evening, some years ago, I became aware of an endless stream of self-criticism flooding my mind as I was returning home at the end of a workday. I hadn't done this; I hadn't done that; I didn't have this; I didn't have that. I should turn my face to the wall in shame. I had no right to exist on this planet, etc. This self-flagellation simply has to stop, I said to myself.

That night I made a list of positive things I had done that day: meditation and prayer in the morning, projects completed or advanced at work, the AA meeting I had attended. That list was an attempt to rein in my negative emotions and achieve some degree of emotional balance.

My sponsor was gentle with me in early recovery. "Why don't you write some of that out?" he would say, when I called him, sometimes three or four times a day, in the throes of fury over some wrong, real or imagined, that had been visited on me by my boss or my wife. But my emotions seemed to burst every dam I sought to construct. Once I had "the goods" on someone, I would go at them with prosecutorial zeal. I had given only cursory attention to resentments in my Fourth Step inventory; I paid a terrible price in not fully grasping that resentment formula in our Big Book: "I'm resentful at ... Affects my ... Where (was I) to blame?"

Today that resentment formula is a staple of my Tenth Step inventory. The surprising durability of the old idea that if someone wins, I lose, makes the formula essential. It is where I go when I am gripped by a recurring bad feeling about someone, whatever the cause. It is an effort to ease the power I have given people over me. Many times I have put pen to paper in a rage at man or woman or God and even as I wrote began to feel this release from emotional turmoil and a shift toward blessed peace. I am like a boiler in need of a safety valve to reduce the risk of explosion, and the Tenth Step is that safety valve. If I am to avoid endlessly recycling slights, affronts, and other personal injuries, then pen and paper become effective tools in leaching this emotional pain from my system. It is on paper that I begin to practice self-honesty, make real progress toward the self-discipline that sobriety requires, and slowly learn to treat others with the courtesy, kindness, justice, and love that the essay in *Twelve Steps and Twelve Traditions* sets as a goal.

Toward that end, I give free rein to my emotions on paper, as it does me no good to censor myself. "I feel X is vile. I feel it would be a happy day if he were to be run over by a bus." Feelings may not be facts, as we say, but they are powerful, and writing out my anger in terms of them is a necessary and cathartic first step. Thereafter, I can try to be specific in terms of the hurt or the injury I feel I have suffered and then further specify what it affects in me—pride, self-esteem, security, etc. Further relief is provided when I ask myself what my part in the difficulty has been. Is it my self-centeredness? My competitiveness? My hypersensitivity? Putting a name to my defects—whether it is envy or jealousy—is an important part of this process. And then prayer. Not once, not twice, but often for a week or even two, praying that this person have the same happiness, prosperity, etc., I wish for myself. It is where I ultimately must go for relief.

Though I do try to list my assets and be mindful of resentment, some emotional disturbance cannot be remedied with a simple formula. In a period of marital crisis, followed by separation and ultimately divorce, I struggled with my core fear—abandonment— and came to understand, through good direction from my sponsor and a therapist, that a terrified child had accompanied me into my adult years, and how that terror had informed some of my objectionable behavior in my home life. I had sought to deny my powerlessness and mask my fear and vulnerability with long stretches of silent scorn or verbal fury.

To access the underlying source of much of my marital pain, I began to write out my inventory in the form of a question-and-answer dialogue between my lower self and higher self. Over time the exercise highlighted the emotional dependency on my mother that had formed in my childhood years and how that had carried over into adult relationships. If the lower self often spoke as a needy, fearful child, the higher self offered comforting, common sense adult perspective. It would remind me that I was no longer back in that family of origin matrix.

With Step Ten, we have entered the world of spirit, and so, inevitably, this Step and Step Eleven are intertwined. Meditation can be like a dredging operation. Buried fears and resentments sometimes rise to the surface and I see what a moment before had been invisible to me.

Step Ten says "when," not "if." Inevitably, I will be in the wrong at some point. That being the case, it is best for me to promptly admit my error. To leave the wrong unaddressed is to allow it to grow and fester. Rationalization, self-justification and rancor thrive the longer I postpone. I may even seek out others to support my "case." And yet, when I become willing to take the simple action required and follow through with an apology or an amend, then I am returned to a state of emotional equilibrium. I have no past or future. I am simply living in the now, where the Higher Power wants me to be. In this regard, an examination of motive is often useful.

"The real war is the war I fight with myself," a man said some years ago. If that is so, then the real victory is over myself and the cruel dictates of my ego: refraining from that face-to-face outburst or waiting 24 hours before dropping that letter in the mailbox. Before letting fly with an oral or written outburst, I can first ask myself these three questions: Is what I say true? Is it kind? Is it necessary? And how many more humiliations must I suffer before I learn to delay hitting the "send" key on a hastily written and inappropriate email?

Journaling may not be a method suitable for everyone. The Steps in large part do become automatic for many of us as we go along, though for me writing is essential as a way of maintaining contact with myself. An inner guide seems to let me know when it is time to put pen to paper. There was a time when I wrote in my journal every day, and perhaps I would be better off if I still did. But now I go to it two or three times a week.

Emotional disturbance can find me at 29 years of recovery as it did when I had 29 minutes. The longer I am sober, the more deeply I am capable of feeling. I have not outgrown fear. I am not so spiritually evolved that I no longer experience resentment.

And sometimes a written inventory is simply to gain clarity on an issue. A simple pros and cons list can do wonders.

Nothing could be sadder than to lose touch with ourselves in recovery: to have our connection to our Higher Power blocked by resentment; to be governed by old ideas we are only dimly if at all aware of and that hold us back; or to be reduced by our fears to living sequestered from life. For the Sunlight of the Spirit to enter, the window must be kept clean so the light can pour through. It's for me to understand that I can pay to have the windows in my apartment cleaned, but that inner window is one that I must tend to. Sponsors and others can be part of the process, but ultimately it is a task for me to perform.

David S.
New York, New York

STEP ELEVEN

"*Sought through prayer and meditation to improve our conscious contact with God as we understood Him, praying only for knowledge of His will for us and the power to carry that out.*"

'm sure I am still very much in the beginner's class," Bill W. wrote about Step Eleven, as he approached his 24th anniversary of sobriety. "Around me I see many people who make a far better job of relating themselves to God than I do. … I haven't made the progress that I might have made." He went on to write that he probably had plenty of company in his lack of attention to this Step. And its neglect, he writes, "can cause us to miss the finest experiences of life."

AA literature points out that there is plenty of written material, inside and outside the program, available for those trying prayer and meditation. *Twelve Steps and Twelve Traditions* suggests the Saint Francis Prayer as a starting point for meditation. "As though lying upon a sunlit beach, let us relax and breathe deeply of the spiritual atmosphere with which the grace of this prayer surrounds us."

AAs who do not practice a Christian religion, or who do not adhere to any faith at all, describe in this chapter's stories how they pray and meditate, and how they realize the peace of mind promised in the AA literature.

"Meditation is our first step out into the sun," the essay on Step Eleven in the "Twelve and Twelve" says. "One of its first fruits is emotional balance."

Still, like Bill, even those who have been sober for many years struggle with prayer and meditation. These AAs' stories reveal the varieties of Step Eleven experiences.

Not Taking the First Drink

October 1978

Around the tables, I quite often state that God's will for me is simply not to take the first drink. This is usually a comment related to the Eleventh Step. I have been told that this is too simple, a cop-out, and several other things. I realize that it is simple, and for me, who suffered (suffer) distorted thinking as a by-product of my alcoholism, simplicity is a necessity.

Going about my day and not taking the first drink require a steady awareness of the good in life. Since God's will for me is not to take the first drink, obviously God's will for me is good. Ever since I learned about the first drink in AA, my life has been one of increasing good. Like Adam and Eve, I have obtained a promise of paradise if I just stay away from this "forbidden fruit." And so I work hard on making certain I don't take the first drink, and the results are delightful.

Never did I accomplish much following my own will. To be exact, my will for me brought disaster; and so I bend my will to the simple task I have each day. The longer and better my sobriety becomes, the more of it I want. Why waste energy in the valueless pursuit of determining God's will as to the brown striped tie or the solid one? Trying to hear and carry out God's will for me is not an occasional chore; it is a full-time, joyous adventure. Thus, I follow the Eleventh Step and work on getting more power to carry out God's will.

Anonymous

Rewards of Meditation

February 1982

From working Step Eleven myself and listening to the experiences of others, I have learned that the ten preceding Steps must be worked before the meditation in Step Eleven can be done with any measure of success. For instance, we should review each day, good and bad (Tenth Step), and make spot-check inventories for moments of emotional tension. After this work is accomplished, meditation can be done—although consistent effort on our part is required.

Immediately upon awakening, I kneel down and pray for sobriety in the coming day and for God's mercy and grace. Then, I say the Third Step Prayer (Big Book, page 63). In repeating the Seventh Step Prayer (Big Book, page 76), I add my own individual character defects, and I also say the Serenity Prayer and a few of our AA slogans.

Now, I am ready to meditate. I select a spot as quiet as possible. Sitting in a comfortable, straight-backed chair with my arms resting on its arms, my feet flat on the floor, and my eyes closed, I begin to repeat to myself over and over again a phrase or a word such as "God is love," "truth," or "Thy will be done." After a while, my mind becomes bored with this repetition, and my thoughts wander to activities planned for the day or what I did yesterday or fears or resentments I may have at the time. I watch these thoughts, so to speak, and eventually get tired of them and automatically return to the phrase or word I had been repeating in the beginning. I say "automatically" now; however, this habit was developed only after repeated practice and effort, a day at a time.

I continue the repetition of the word or phrase to myself. I become bored again and my mind wanders again, and so the process goes. I try to meditate effortlessly. I try to relax. If I itch, I scratch where it itches. If my position in the chair becomes uncomfortable, I change it. If noise occurs, I accept it calmly and just continue my meditation. I may intersperse some of the prayers repeated earlier into this meditation. Whether, in my opinion, I am meditating well or not, I continue. My willingness to try to seek God's will and gain more sanity is the most important thing. As Thomas Merton said in his last book, *Contemplative Prayer,* "A hard and apparently fruitless meditation may in fact be much more valuable than one that is easy, happy, enlightened, and apparently a big success."

After almost six and a half years of sobriety, my meditation amounts to two thirty-five-minute periods, one upon awakening, the other in late afternoon. When I started meditation, four years ago or so, I had great difficulty sitting still for even five minutes. I wasn't disciplined enough. I was nervous and fidgety and couldn't slow my mind down. Only through repeatedly trying to meditate twice a day every day (missing only a few times) was I able to achieve the self-discipline to sit still longer.

I continue to practice Step Eleven throughout the day. I often repeat the Third and Seventh Step Prayers silently or out loud, to myself or on the phone and in person with other AAs who do this kind of work. I talk to God. I practice his presence in my life, trying to improve conscious contact with him. When walking to and from work and at other times during the day, I may repeat the words "Thy will be done" for every four steps I take—one word for one step. This is a convenient discipline and provides another opportunity for conscious contact with my Higher Power.

The result of all this Eleventh Step work is a greater willingness to accept life for what it is, to deal with reality instead of rationalizing the way I want it to be. Periods of serenity occur more often, and so do thoughts of others. Overwhelming self-concern is reduced. The feeling that things will work out as long as I stay sober becomes stronger. The thought that God's will really is the answer for my life comes to mind more frequently.

As the "Twelve and Twelve" says (page 105), "Perhaps one of the greatest rewards of meditation and prayer is the sense of belonging that comes to us. We no longer live in a completely hostile world. We are no longer lost and frightened and purposeless. The moment we catch even a glimpse of God's will, the moment we begin to see truth, justice and love as the real and eternal things in life, we are no longer deeply disturbed by all the seeming evidence to the contrary that surrounds us in purely human affairs. We know that when we turn to Him, all will be well with us, here and hereafter."

This practicing of the Eleventh Step, along with reworking all the other Steps, has given me greater integrity and strengthened my sobriety. This is the kind of dependence I need: a healthy and sure dependence on the Twelve Steps. Step Eleven has shown me real benefits. It will continue to do so if I just work at it, a day at a time.

S.M.
Joliet, Illinois

Freeing the Spirit

February 1984

One of the key ideas, it seems to me, in the successful practice of the Twelve Steps as a recovery program is contained in the words "conscious contact." The only way I could arrive at any degree of consciousness regarding the physical and the mental/emotional aspects of my recovery, and of my alcoholism itself, was through application of the first ten Steps. Also very helpful was jumping over the fence and making excursions into the Twelfth.

Approaching the Eleventh, then, I already had a good working knowledge of the limitations imposed on me by my threefold disease. That degree of awareness provided a comfortable lead-in to an understanding of the third aspect of alcoholism, the spiritual. Time was, whenever I'd be called on at an AA meeting to share on this Step, I'd become a guru and soar into guruland. I didn't share my experience; I taught a lesson on spirituality, a how-you-too-can-become-spiritual lesson. (In my early AA years, it was called "pontificating"—but only if someone else did it!)

I see my drinking years, for the most part, as a prolonged effort to improve my conscious contact with reality and with a Power greater than reality. Occasional insight told me that drinking was not the best way. Yet I could cite bands of men and women down through the ages who had practiced severe mortification of the flesh in their pursuit of contact with something beyond ordinary attainment. That was their way, I told myself, and drinking was mine. Alcohol seemed to open doors to a high spiritual life that remained beyond my mortal reach.

Before coming to AA, I spent upwards of two years in psychoanalysis, a therapy that helped a great deal with many of my problems. With my one major problem, however—alcoholism—it offered no practical help whatsoever. My analyst once made an observation that was beyond my understanding at the time but stayed with me, perhaps because of the mystery it posed. In response to my frequent complaints about a fire in my innards, she asked me whether I had ever poured kerosene into a lighted stove. The result, she said, would be similar to pouring spirits on a spiritual fire—conflagration!

What was the source, or cause, of that spiritual fire? I don't really know. Down through my sober years thus far, I have been satisfied to think of it as a manifestation of longing for reunion with something—in AA, we call it a Power greater than ourselves. Some of us call it God.

Once, at a Step meeting, a woman told of her return to church in the belief that it was the only way her prayers would be heard. On her first visit, she was quite surprised to find people there. She had long ago concluded that nobody went to church anymore. Now, she had become a regular churchgoer. For her, church was the most comfortable place for praying.

I was unable to accept churchgoing in my early AA years; so I sought other kinds of help in working this Step. There are certain books promoting peace of mind that I enjoy reading. Perhaps the most attractive book as an aid to meditation is our own Conference-approved reader, *As Bill Sees It*.

Recently, I spent a ten-month period eleventh-stepping myself. My objective was to find out whether I was working at the right job, or whether I should be using my God-given talents in another capacity. I felt I knew what I wanted to do, but because I had been trapped in one job for a very long time, I was no longer sure I could distinguish between wishful thinking and intuition.

During the day or as I lay in bed at night, I'd repeat the words of the Step, each time emphasizing and dwelling on different ones.

What came of that eleventh-stepping adventure? From an unexpected source, I was summoned to a job interview. No, I didn't get the job; but that interview led to another, and this time I did get the job. It was the kind of work I had long believed I wanted to do, with the very organization I most wanted to work with. Happy ending, with the Eleventh Step to thank? No. I was fired. How come? I wasn't equal to the job. Apparently, I had misread God's will for me. Then, it became a matter of praying for the power to accept what I've heard some AAs refer to as not a spiritual awakening but a rude awakening!

Just as the earlier Steps had granted me physical freedom from alcohol and mental/emotional freedom from the stigma of alcoholism, so did my introduction to Step Eleven represent an unprecedented experiment in freedom of the spirit. No longer would I have to say, "Get me out of this mess, and I'll never do such and such again." No more bargaining, no more dictating, no more all-or-nothing! Thy will, not mine, be done!

Incidentally, there are ways other than prayer and meditation by which I can continue to improve my conscious contact with a Power greater than myself—for example, sharing in the maiden talk of a newcomer, rejoicing at the return of a member who has relapsed, and (not to be underestimated) the continuing wonder of waking up each morning sober.

"Quiet times" are of huge value to me. As recounted in *Dr. Bob and the Good Oldtimers*, AA's co-founder practiced a quiet time of from thirty minutes to an hour every morning, when he read from inspirational books and meditated, a practice he continued into his later years.

In a piece that our other co-founder, Bill W., wrote for the Grapevine (June 1958), he said, "I've just finished rereading the chapter on Step Eleven in our book *Twelve Steps and Twelve Traditions*. This was written almost five years ago. I was astonished when I realized how little time I had actually been giving to my own elementary advice on meditation, prayer, and guidance—practices that I had so earnestly recommended to everybody else!"

It still amazes me that those two men who bore the burden of our pioneer years continued to believe and to work at improving their conscious contact with a Power greater than themselves. And all the other early members who carried the AA message the length and breadth of the land—before the Eleventh Step was written, they, too, relied on a Power greater than themselves. They, too, prayed for knowledge of his will and for the power to follow through.

The Step worked for them in those days, and it works for me today. There is not the slightest doubt in my mind that it will work for all those alcoholics yet to come through our doors. But as always, "First Things First." Before we can release the spirit from its imprisonment, we must first imprison the spirits in the bottle. We place the bottle on the shelf, place ourselves in the hands of AA as we understand it, and prepare for the adventure of sobriety. For me, it's an adventure unthought of and undreamed of in all the years of my drinking life.

W.H.
Manhattan, New York

Should We Go Easy on the God Stuff?

April 2002

In a recent online AA meeting I participate in, someone posed the question, "Why do we hear, 'Go easy on the God stuff' at AA meetings, so we don't scare off the new person?" "After all," he reasoned, "if AA is all about God, why should we soft-peddle AA's core principle?" Here's my response to this topic.

Bill W.'s first draft of the Twelve Steps—which originally numbered only six steps— spoke of God without the expansive descriptions "as we understand Him" or "a power greater than ourselves." I am convinced that if Bill had not subsequently qualified God as "a power greater than ourselves," and "God as we understood him," Alcoholics Anonymous may very well have become the alcoholic squadron of the Oxford Group instead of a worldwide movement embraced by people of all religious traditions in over 150 countries. In the 1920s, the Oxford Group counted about one million members worldwide. Try reaching the closest chapter of the Oxford Group on the phone today.

I am equally convinced that a twelve-step program based exclusively on Christianity, or with any similar sectarian underpinning, would be of limited value to the still-suffering alcoholic. Organized religion, especially in the West, cannot help being structurally sectarian because it must distinguish between its ultimate truths and the beliefs of other faiths.

Several years ago, an alcoholic told me that he had stopped attending AA meetings because our program felt like recycled Christianity. I think that this person's spirituality was rooted in Hinduism, or at least in Raja Yoga, and he was put off by the frequent references to the Christian deity in meetings. At the time, I took exception to the idea that AA was a Christian organization, but I have come to appreciate how he formed such an opinion.

Where I live, in southeastern Virginia, it seems that the people in meetings most interested in talking about their God are fundamentalist Christians—many of whom fervently believe they possess the exclusive ticket to salvation, and that you are doomed unless you share their beliefs. Fundamentalists feel compelled to witness in the hope of saving those who might otherwise miss the salvation express. Their parochial presentation of God lacks the ecumenical view outlined by Bill W. that is the foundation of Alcoholics Anonymous.

While the Hindu tradition has literally hundreds of gods, there are other widely held spiritual beliefs that are nondeistic—they do not put forth belief in a deity as essential to the faith. Taoism and Buddhism are two such examples. Our basic text, *Alcoholics Anonymous,* talks about people from different religious and spiritual traditions in Chapter 4, "We Agnostics":

"When, therefore, we speak to you of God, we mean your own conception of God. This applies too, to other spiritual expressions which you find in this book."

In Chapter 7, "Working With Others," the Big Book gives sage advice that directly speaks to the question of what to tell newcomers about God and spirituality:

"Tell him exactly what happened to you. Stress the spiritual feature freely. If the man be agnostic or atheist, make it emphatic that he does not have to agree with your conception of God. He can choose any conception he likes, provided it makes sense to him. The main thing is that he be willing to believe in a Power greater than himself and that he live by spiritual principles."

All that AA suggests is that someone be willing to believe in a power greater than one's self and be willing to live by spiritual principles. The Big Book outlines our straightforward choice: "To be doomed to an alcoholic death or to live on a spiritual basis are not always easy alternatives to face." If AA had required that I believe in the God of my childhood, I would have been thoroughly screwed because, for me, that notion of God died long ago. Thanks to AA, my personal spirituality is the vital center of my life today. I believe that there are innumerable paths to God—including all the sects of the Christian faith.

Bill W.'s personal story in the Big Book informs us that, after reading William James's *Varieties of Religious Experience,* he was still unable to make the essential spiritual connection due to lingering antipathy for his childhood God. It was only when Ebby suggested what seemed like a novel idea—"Why don't you choose your own conception of God?"—that Bill W. was open to receive the Sunlight of the Spirit: "That statement hit me hard. It melted the icy intellectual mountain in whose shadow I had lived and shivered many years. I stood in the sunlight at last.

"It was only a matter of being willing to believe in a Power greater than myself. Nothing more was required of me to make my beginning. I saw that growth could start from that point. Upon a foundation of complete willingness I might build what I saw in my friend. Would I have it? Of course I would!"

Like Bill W., when I came into the Fellowship, I was just barely capable of sweeping generalities about a higher power, like Universal Mind, Spirit of Nature, or First Cause; however, these limited conceptions were sufficient to establish a beachhead from which to start the spiritual journey of recovery. If I were to come to AA today for the first time and hear a lot of talk about Jesus versus a Power greater than myself, I don't know if I'd stay around for the miracle. Thanks for encouraging me to follow my personal spiritual path since 1982.

Doug B.
Virginia

Clean Slate

February 2009

After being in AA for over twelve years, something was amiss. I still wasn't "right" with myself. At an Eleventh Step meeting, I discovered what was wrong.

I wanted love, yet felt anger and hate. I wanted peace, but felt anxious and fearful. I wanted faith, but I didn't trust or believe in people or God.

I love the prayer of St. Francis, the "Eleventh Step Prayer." I had to rethink the way I acted out the prayer. We are all born with a clean slate and no obvious character defects. We go through life picking up bad habits and doing wrong things. Add alcohol to the fray and what do I have? A bonafide defect looking for character. Okay, so I get sober, do all these changes for myself so that I may join the human race. Now I think I'm ready to join St. Francis as an instrument of peace! The reality is that St. Francis is at the end of the road, his hands on his hips, waiting for me to go on the journey with him.

If I remove my hate and anger, what is left is love. If I remove my anxiety and fear, peace will result. If I believe in God's promises, the obstacles that I created between God and myself will be lifted. When these defects are removed, then I can start to be an instrument of peace.

John M.
Chicago, Illinois

From Foxhole to Light

March 2008

My journey through recovery has been filled with rewards—gifts from my Higher Power. None of them, however, came without hard work, but the most arduous was practicing the Eleventh Step as it applied to my relationship with my son.

He was an active alcoholic by the age of thirteen. On his sixteenth birthday, he left our recovering household, dragged helplessly downward by the condition he was powerless over. Rarely have I seen a case get so severe so quickly. In a short time, he was homeless. Months would go by without a word from him. Every time the phone rang, I feared it was the police calling to tell us that his body had been found, burned beyond recognition, or asphyxiated on his own vomit, or beaten to death in a bar he had slipped into underage.

I was surrounded by many good, stable, recovering people, all of whom verified that I was not overreacting, but assured me that the working of the Steps and loving support of the Fellowship would carry me through, should any of those horrible scenarios actually occur. I worked hard at keeping my own recovery on track, but nothing prepared me for the day my sponsor challenged me with the most radical course of action I had ever heard. He proposed: "Why don't you stop praying for him?"

I was stunned. I had a religious background and I'd always believed in God, although I arrived at our Fellowship with what I call today "a God as I misunderstood him." I thought of God as a sort of spiritual vending machine, and prayer was the coin I used to try to buy—or at least bribe—from God the things I desired. I had spent years in the Fellowship believing that the Eleventh Step instructed me to pray for "knowledge of his will for us and the power to carry that out." But I had missed the key word in that Step, which it took a loving, but firm, sponsor to point out: the word "only."

I had spent a lifetime saying foxhole prayers, mostly along the lines of, "Please get me out of this and I'll do anything." My sponsor confronted me with the reality that those prayers had been answered, and I now had some responsibilities to face. Having been rescued from a living hell, it was now time to put my money where my mouth was. There was to be no cheating and no rewriting of the Steps to suit my own convenience. Step Eleven did not say, "praying only for my son to get sober, as well as knowledge of God's will and the power to carry it out." If I were serious about my recovery, it was time to work the Step as written. I was to begin, that day, to ask God for nothing but direction. I had to accept the reality of the situation, instead of begging God to change it. From that day forth, my prayer changed from "Please get my son sober" to "Please show me how to best parent a dying child."

For the next four years, I gritted my teeth during prayer, resisting the urge to beg God for my son's life. Soon, as a direct result of my proper application of this Step, an amazing thing occurred: my son's illness got worse and worse, but our relationship got better and better. The atmosphere between us changed from one fraught with tension (because of my terror of what would happen if he didn't change) to one of mercy, love, and, once again, respect. Instead of hiding from me for months at a time, he called me regularly and we went for walks together. He poured out his woes to me, saying, "I know it's the drinking, I know I should stop, but I just can't." Instead of whipping out a meeting schedule, or a pamphlet from the best treatment center around, I would just put my arm around his shoulder and say, "I know you can't, but remember I'll always love you and be here for you, whether you can stop or not."

What I had not realized was that as long as I was fighting God for things to be different than they were, I was subtly, or not so subtly, giving my son the same message—demanding from a sick, dying child that he do something that Step One should have reminded me he was powerless to do: stop drinking. He could no more abstain than a crippled child could walk. My pressure on him, which I hadn't even been aware of, was making me unapproachable to the frightened and lonely child buried underneath the ugliness of a young man's addiction. If the worst had happened, how unimaginable my grief would have been the day I realized my child died alone, unable to cry out to me for comfort because the impossible expectations of his fear-driven father had created a wedge between us.

I sat proudly next to my son at an AA meeting this morning. It has been several years since he called me on the morning of Father's Day and asked me to get him help. I brought him to a treatment center, and when I picked him up, weeks later, I gave him a ride to a meeting, hugged him, and said, "You're on your own now." I gave him the dignity to find his own way without piggy-backing onto the network of his family's recovery circle.

Please don't mistake the message I conclude with: My finally getting the Eleventh Step right didn't get him sober. My son rose to the challenge by the grace of God and the Fellowship of Alcoholics Anonymous, not because his father finally got the message he'd been reading since the day of his first meeting many years before. The Big Book says, "No human power could have relieved our alcoholism, but God could and would if he were sought." How wonderful it feels, though, that when my boy's moment of truth came, he knew he could always call his Dad.

Mike D.
Syracuse, New York

Finding My Way

April 2009

I denounced the Christianity of my upbringing sometime around age 15. As my interest in history, world cultures and social activism grew, so did my skepticism regarding Christianity. I didn't seek out a different spiritual path, I just put any thoughts of spirituality out of my mind, except when I read about people of a spiritual nature. By the time I was 16, my budding alcoholism took off full force. My only real interest was the obsession to drink as often as possible and the typical 16-year-old boy stuff like girls and music. Sometimes in a drunken stupor I would talk about theology or philosophy, which isn't a good thing to do when trying to attract someone of the opposite sex. I called myself an atheist, but in reality I was an agnostic or a theosophist, like Voltaire.

I believed in something but wasn't sure what it was.

In 1982, during a period of mandatory abstinence from alcohol, thanks to the U.S. Air Force, I was hiking by myself in the Rocky Mountains. I stopped to rest on an outcrop of rock overlooking a vast valley. My eyes were opened to all the amazing colors and formations; my ears were open to a multitude of sounds. I smelled the earth, air, vegetation and everything else. My mind was opened to a belief in a divine creator, one that created nature. It was on this outcrop of rock that I had my first spiritual experience.

Fast-forward five years. The combination of fear, loneliness and depression—fueled by heavy daily drinking—brought my shuffling feet through the door of an AA meeting. I honestly don't remember much about those first few meetings, other than that the guys there seemed really happy. They were openly talking about their feelings and complications in life and how they dealt with them without drinking. They understood the alcohol-induced depression I was living in and they offered me hope. The other thing I noticed was that the Third and Eleventh Steps said: "God as we understood Him." Cool—finally a group that would allow me to believe in my own concept of God.

Over the course of my next years of continuous sobriety, my spirituality didn't grow much beyond my belief in a divine force in the universe. I would say a prayer of thanks in the morning and before I went to sleep. I would say a pray of thanks when even the smallest good fortune came my way, like a green light when I really needed one. I said the Serenity Prayer to help me calm down in tense situations, but that was pretty much it. I never took a close look at the Eleventh Step, nor truly added it to my daily practice of recovery.

I attended meetings in small towns in rural Nebraska. Bit by bit I started getting resentful toward people who used the Christian-implied concept of God too much when they shared. If someone talked about Jesus too much, I would be filled with unspoken rage. I was afraid to tell anyone my feelings. I figured no one would understand or they would try to sway my beliefs toward theirs. AA was my safe haven and my only social life, so I sure didn't want to risk losing it. Something was happening inside me that I wasn't aware of—the Big Book talks about it. I was becoming that dry drunk who would give anything to take a couple of drinks and get away with it. At meetings I was happy and friendly, but really, I was whistling in the dark. I wasn't happy in AA; my marriage was a mess; I had financial troubles; I wasn't really happy with my job; and, since I was a member of the Air Guard, I was hanging around people who "drank with impunity." I reached the jumping-off point, picked up a six-pack of beer and jumped. I didn't land for 10 years and then it was at a treatment center. I didn't land on my feet either, I might add.

In my first few months back in active recovery and regular attendance at AA meetings, I was comfortable being reunited with the God of my understanding. But it took a big lesson in comparing my insides with other's outsides for this to happen. Understanding my perceptions can be a great butt-kicking too. Something inside of me was telling me I needed more. This time I heard the voice and heeded it.

When I read the Eleventh Step in the "Twelve and Twelve," the Prayer of St. Francis really struck me hard and I had an awakening. I was sure I had read it a few times before in my past life of recovery, but wasn't ready to hear the message. Even though the prayer was written by a Christian man, I saw it in an Eastern religious light.

I have always had an interest in Taoism and Buddhism, but other than reading the Tao a few times, I never looked deeper at either one. So with my new personal interpretation of the St. Francis Prayer, I set out to explore Buddhism. In doing so, the Eleventh Step came to life for me. Thanks to my new willingness, I began a spiritual journey.

By incorporating basic Buddhist practices with my AA practices—regular meetings, doing service, working with newcomers, living the Steps and reading AA literature—I have discovered an awesome way to improve my conscious contact with the God of my understanding and live life on life's terms in relative serenity. I still have anxieties, anger and all the rest of the emotions that come with life, but, bit by bit, I am able to manage them.

My concept of God hasn't changed much since I sat on that mountain outcrop, but my spirituality has. This is thanks to working all the Steps this time around and not leaving out the Eleventh. Using a combination of what is written in the Big Book and the Prayer of St. Francis, and an effort toward unselfishness, compassion and right mindfulness—and right speech, right view, right intentions, right livelihood, right concentration, right effort and right action—I am aware of my inner self and how it affects me and those I come in contact with, and what I need to do to improve my way of thinking and acting. I have faith that as long as I do these things, I won't reach that jumping-off place again

Scott W.

Kearney, Nebraska

Alcoholic's Meditation

November 2010 (Dear Grapevine)

After several years of regular attendance at an Eleventh Step study, a simple meditation came to me that I think of as the "alcoholic's meditation." With each in-breath, I think, Welcome. With each out-breath, I think, Thank you. That leaves me fluctuating between acceptance and gratitude, which I recognize as two of the integral principles of Alcoholics Anonymous. Although my sobriety is based on faith in God, this simple meditation can work for agnostics and atheists as well, who can readily practice acceptance and gratitude without necessarily believing in God. Like so many things in AA, this meditation works when I work it. By welcoming God into my day and then thanking him for being in it, this meditation continually blesses me.

Ed L.
Wrightwood, California

STEP TWELVE

"Having had a spiritual awakening as the result of these steps, we tried to carry this message to alcoholics, and to practice these principles in all our affairs."

Sharing your story at a meeting. Setting up coffee. Putting chairs away after the meeting. Taking a meeting into a jail or other institution. All of these Twelfth Step activities can be as important as driving a drunk to a detox while introducing him to the program.

Yet the first "Twelfth-Step call" with an active alcoholic can be profound, an eye-opening experience to a newly sober AA, especially one still doubting his commitment to sobriety.

Intensive work with other alcoholics, time after time, helps provide immunity from drinking. This is part of the "spiritual awakening" mentioned in the Step.

How does an AA recognize that he has had a "spiritual awakening"? "He has now become able to do, feel, and believe that which he could not do before on his unaided strength of resources alone," the "Twelve and Twelve" says.

"Two things are involved in the Twelfth Step: the spread of the awakening to others, and the deepening and continuation of the awakening in ourselves," Dr. Samuel Shoemaker, the widely known Episcopal clergyman who helped in the founding of AA, wrote in the January 1964 Grapevine.

The success of AA lies in its members' readiness to go to any lengths to help other alcoholics, Dr. Shoemaker wrote. "Now we must begin to look wide without, concern ourselves with individuals, causes, communities and the wider worlds. Here is the secret of growth and spread."

Carrying the Message

April 1971

If you are like I am and would rather gain than lose a few meetings while on vacation, you might play the game that my wife and I play. We call it AA-hopping, and it is just like bar-hopping, only different.

We pack our clothes, fill the car with gas, and take the group directory along. We then drive until we get tired, find lodgings, look in the directory, and call a friend we have never met—who "just happens to be sitting by the phone awaiting our call." He or she gives us the local AA picture and takes us to a meeting.

We have just returned from such a trip, where we shared our experience, strength, and hope with a number of groups in the western half of two states, plus a mini-visit to a "foreign" country. I can't see any difference between the lovable alkies of Victoria and the guys and gals at home.

I highly recommend this kind of vacation and feel that we have gained a lot while doing a little Twelfth Step work.

Anonymous
Brookings, Oregon

Practice the Principles

June 1981

Around the tables, when we talk about the Twelfth Step, more often than not it is in terms of twelfth-stepping—that is, helping newcomers to AA. Naturally, some attention is focused on the other aspects of the Step, namely, the spiritual awakening and the practice of AA principles in all our affairs. But do we go into those aspects as deeply as we should?

I have recently been receiving a number of pointed reminders about the practice of principles. It is easy to practice principles at AA meetings and in meditation times at home; but once out the door, it is another matter.

I must admit also that I sometimes stumble about the principles right at an AA meeting. As a matter of fact, even in the quiet times, early in the morning, I can catch myself reflecting on someone else's defects and shortcomings. Fortunately, as sobriety lengthens and more meetings are attended, I am getting better—just as promised if I didn't take that first drink.

Each morning now, often during the day, I ask for help in my efforts to make the quiet meditation times a basis for practicing AA principles in all my affairs that day. Simply asking for help seems to be a help in itself; with this seeking, life becomes more beautiful and exciting. Others may not realize yet that I am trying to practice AA principles in all my affairs, but I know I am trying. Most important, I realize I need help to do so. That means I am coming to grips with my ego. When I do, I go out the door—and find people much easier to deal with.

Anonymous

The Woman Who Had Everything

December 1993

Forty-eight years ago I took the First Step to get into AA. But it was the Twelfth Step that kept me there.

In the Big Book of Alcoholics Anonymous, Bill W. said, "For me to stay sober, I had to help alcoholics to get sober." That is the Twelfth Step. In those days I had little or no faith, but Bill was a living example that I had to believe.

For the next five years, everyone who came my way got the Twelfth Step treatment whether they wanted it or not. In time I lightened up a bit and began to make friends who have lasted for years.

While I was involved with helping someone stay sober, I forgot I was extremely self-conscious, forgot to feel inferior, worthless, and useless.

One day while I was volunteering at the clubhouse, a call came for someone to take a woman to the hospital. She was in desperate shape and it must be as soon as possible. I said, "I'll go."

In Maria Louise's duplex apartment, I saw a whole new world. I had never seen anything like it—unless maybe in the movies. There was beautiful French period furniture, crystal chandeliers, a magnificent Chinese rug. It was a sight to behold.

It was also a scene right out of a Tennessee Williams play: a once-beautiful blonde in a state of frantic despair and fighting mad. Across the room there sat her little mother on a blue satin loveseat. She was holding her daughter's suitcase on her lap, trying to be helpful in a hopeless situation. I had always believed I was an alcoholic because my mother had died when I was three, because my father made me leave home when I was fourteen at his new wife's request, because my family wasn't affluent—and here I was faced with a young woman who had everything. She had her mother and a beautiful home and wealth. And that didn't give Maria Louise sobriety. That instant changed my thinking about the causes of my alcoholism.

After a while, Maria Louise was persuaded to get in a taxi and go to a posh Eastside hospital. After she was put to bed and was medicated, the nurse gave me the responsibility for seeing that she drank orange juice almost constantly. It was part of the treatment.

I sat by her from four in the afternoon until one in the morning. It was an important opportunity to care for someone with all my heart, body, and soul. As a reward I had a warm good feeling that I shall always treasure. That was the beginning of a new good life for me.

Nancy
Kennett Square, Pennsylvania

Got It? Give It. Forget It!

December 1998

It would be virtually impossible to experience the Twelve Steps and not learn something of love. I believe that love is the willingness to extend oneself for spiritual growth. When we answer a call for help, we are extending ourselves for the purpose of spiritual growth. Someone once said that there are three steps to becoming a loving person: love yourself, be yourself, forget yourself. Proper Twelfth Step work requires a forgetting of self.

Sometimes, in sponsoring, I forget to listen. Active listening can be twelfth-stepping. Listening is an act of love.

I cannot honestly say that I came into AA initially to stop drinking. I came seeking happiness. I soon learned that I didn't stand a chance for happiness unless I first got sober. Having had some rich experiences in the Steps, I've learned that we create our own happiness to the degree that we contribute to the comfort and happiness of others. The best way to have happiness is to give it.

Albert Schweitzer expressed it very profoundly: "I don't know what your destiny will be, but one thing I know; the only ones among you who will be truly happy are those who will have sought and found how to serve."

Ed H.
Brentwood, New York

The Luck of the Draw

June 2002

About a year ago, I was able to begin some Twelfth-Step work in a local jail. I think my underlying motive was survivor's guilt; I just hadn't got caught. As I began the work, I realized I had a prejudice that the ladies there had a different, more severe type of alcoholism than I suffered from. There was also a tendency on my part to include the spicier parts of my story.

Boy, was I wrong! It truly is the case that these women are "serving my sentence." The folks in these facilities have the same type of alcoholism that I have. I have noticed that other women who have come in to tell their stories have had similar responses. And on the way out, they realize that it was the luck of the draw, not superior intelligence, that separates the alcoholic inside the walls from those outside.

This service has helped me stay sober more than I thought it would, as well as offering the joy of giving it away. It has certainly altered the inside job my Higher Power has done for me. It also brings home that when we take the first drink, the world can do to us as it sees fit. Our freedom to choose is gone.

Nancy R.
Akron, Ohio

How to Give a Lead

July 2005

I was encouraged to give the lead at my home group. It is a rite of passage, I was told, a part of the Twelfth Step. I said I would think about it.

I am a lousy speaker. Sometimes I forget to breathe, and in the middle of a sentence, I have to gulp for air or turn blue. Sometimes saliva runs down the corners of my mouth like the spittle on an old man.

No, no way. But it happened anyway. I am not good at thinking on my feet; giving an ad-lib speech is beyond my limits and wishes. My lead has to be perfect—one that rocks the rafters and leaves the listeners awestruck. I would have to outline my lead, write it down, transfer it to index cards, memorize and practice, know when to throw in a little humor to lighten my deep thoughts; all the time building hurdles that I couldn't jump even if I were bourbon-reinforced.

I was embarrassed at my story. It was dull. In the first Steps of recovery, as I took personal and moral inventory and made amends, even I was bored. I was just a drunk who drank too much and did not care. I knew that drinking was a slow death, but I was in no hurry.

I didn't start drinking at the age of ten, was never beaten or molested, never jailed, never stole a police car and drove 110 miles an hour down the expressway the wrong way, never lost a wife or children, never had my parents change the locks on the door. I'd done nothing no one hadn't heard before. Somebody's boring and I think it's me.

One evening the guest lead speaker couldn't make the meeting. The chair looked around the room, asking if there was anyone who had never given a lead. No matter how small I shrank in my chair and stared at the ceiling, I couldn't hide.

Okay. Since God got me to AA, certainly he wouldn't let me down now. He didn't.

I stumbled, I rambled, I hemmed and hawed. I said, "Oh, I forgot to tell the part about ... " and wiped the spit from my mouth.

Then God came through. I wasn't giving a speech to a crowd. I was talking to friends in my living room. They were listening to me! They were interested and they cared. I was so excited at being useful that I forgot to be frightened.

At the end, there was applause. A veteran member came to me and said, "I've never heard a lead given just that way."

I took it as a compliment.

Ron B.
Harrison, Ohio

E-Stepping: Carrying the Message Online

December 2005

Y ou should have seen the funny looks I used to get four years ago when I talked about doing Twelfth-Step work online. The old-timers especially used to look at me as if I were nuts. But with time, we learned that while nothing will replace the face-to-face Twelfth-Step call, the language of the heart can be transmitted, no matter what the media—as long as we know what we are talking about, how AA works, and how we can carry the message of AA to the person who is desperate to find a solution. In other words, as long as we have experience, strength and hope.

I am a member involved in the Twelfth-Step Online Committee of Online Intergroup (or "Steppers," as we affectionately call ourselves). Approximately four years ago, we started with one Twelfth-Step "button" on the Online Intergroup website, www.aa-intergroup.org. Currently thirty-six websites based all over the world have a "button" or a link to Steppers, including Belarus, South Africa, Australia, Brazil, France, Canada, and the United States. Our newest member is from McMurdo Station, Antarctica. Length of sobriety among Steppers ranges from several years to thirty, and every Stepper I know attends meetings regularly.

Since our beginning, we have been contacted by an estimated 5,000 people and by 1,297 in the past year alone. There is almost always someone on the committee who speaks one of the common languages on the globe, including some African dialects.

Some want help to stop drinking. Others are traveling and want to know where meetings are located. Still others know people with drinking problems and inquire what they can do as a family member or friend. Everyone's anonymity is respected and the Traditions are taken seriously. And we always recommend that people go to face-to-face meetings and give them help finding those meetings. While we cannot take anyone to a meeting due to sheer distances, we do share experience, strength, and hope just as we would do if someone walked in off the street. We have a vast amount of resources available to pass along.

Some AAs perform great service to the Fellowship by doing face-to-face Twelfth-Step work. Some help by being GSRs or DCMs. Others make coffee and clean the clubs. Some visit jails and schools and develop public service announcements. Still others carry the message from a keyboard. It not only helps us keep sober ourselves, but also may just help the alcoholic find the help he or she needs.

I know several people who have found AA online and begun their sobriety there. A man from Germany who initially contacted us online has been sober now almost three years. He has developed a healthy AA program and continues to work hard. One day we received an email for help from a cruise ship. It was the middle of the night for those passengers. An AA member could not find any "friend of Bill W." on board, so she knocked at the Captain's door to ask for help because she wanted to have a drink. The Captain thought of going online to ask for help and reached one of our buttons, wrote to us, and within minutes, Steppers replied. By morning, this woman had twenty or so replies and had made it through the night without drinking.

M.E.
Flower Mound, Texas

Memory Motel

March 2007

M y first few months of recovery in AA were a flurry of activity. I went to meetings every day, talked to my sponsor constantly, and did lots of service in my home group. But the idea of participating in a traditional Twelfth Step call frightened me. I didn't know anything and barely understood how I'd gotten to Alcoholics Anonymous. What kind of message could I carry to anyone else if I was just beginning to understand it myself?

John, a gentle and caring sober member I'd met, called one morning and asked me to accompany him on a call. A man holed up in a room at a ramshackle motel out on the highway had called the office, he said. He wanted to talk to some guys who were sober.

"This old boy is drinking out there at the motel, and I doubt if he seriously wants to get sober," John said. "But he made the call, and we need to go."

Immediately, the old fear pulsed through me. I stammered out a couple of lame excuses in an attempt to wriggle out of it, but John, in a firm yet understanding way, wouldn't take no for an answer. Somewhere in my mind, I kept hearing the charge: "I am responsible." Before I had more time to worry, we were on our way.

Recovery had opened me up to many interests, and in my newfound sobriety, I found AA's history inspiring. The story of AA Number Three, twelfth-stepped in the hospital by Bill W. and Dr. Bob, came to life in my imagination when I saw the painting, "The Man on the Bed." My first look at that scene filled me with awe. The picture depicted the moment of a miracle—the process that had saved my life and makes AA work. Now, I was on my way to that kind of meeting, walking the same Twelfth Step path as Bill and Dr. Bob. We arrived at the motel and asked the desk clerk where we could find our man. Shaking in my shoes, I followed John to the motel room door.

He knocked hard; a muffled voice came from the other side. John pushed the door open, and the scene in the tiny room astonished me. In front of us was an unmade bed, two chairs, a nightstand, an almost empty bottle, and a man in his undershirt, sitting on the edge of the bed.

We pulled up two chairs and sat down in front of him. His name was Ben, he said, and he had just been released from the local hospital's detox, where he'd been many times before. The nightstand was covered with an array of bottled pills. Ben sipped booze from a large plastic cup. We introduced ourselves, and then Ben talked.

My fear of the situation dissipated as I listened to Ben's tales of misery. He'd had it all, he said. The wife, the kids, the house, the car and the job—all of it. But everything had been gone for a long time. He had tried everything in his attempts to stop drinking, from doctors to religion. Once, he even tried AA and was sober for a short time. But he just couldn't stay with it. The Steps asked too much of him, he said. Sponsors were a bother and annoyance, and the whole thing took too much of his time. But even so, Ben said, he knew the program was something special, and he missed the people and the fellowship. He knew that if he called AA, someone would come.

He talked for a long time; occasionally, John made short comments. I never said a word—I was hypnotized by the scene before me. Finally, Ben wound down.

"How long have you been sober?" he asked John.

"Twelve years, now," John said.

A shadow of sorts crossed Ben's face. He turned to me. "What about you, Don? How long have you been sober?"

At that instant, I felt like Ben's brother. There was only one thing to tell him, and that was the truth.

"Well, Ben, if I make it two more days," I said, "I'll have eight months of sobriety."

The shadow across his face vanished. He raised an eyebrow, and the spark of a twinkle came into his eyes. The corners of his mouth turned up slightly.

"Man, how in the world did you ever do that?" he asked.

The only answers I knew were the truth of my own experience—without exaggeration, embellishment or preaching. My answer came straight from my heart.

"One day at a time, Ben," I said. "I did it one day at a time." The connection, for that moment, was one of pure honesty. Ben wanted to know everything. What had I been like? What had I lost? How did I get to AA? What things did my sponsor "make" me do? With our eyes fixed on each other, I stumbled through some answers.

"Yeah, me too," he said several times. Ben seemed hypnotized as my short tale tumbled out. I was startled by how he'd latched on to me. Suddenly, I realized that John's twelve years of sobriety was too much for Ben to fathom. It had passed right over his head. But he understood and related to me having eight months without a drink. I was more like him. I stumbled through some answers, telling Ben the highlights of my recovery in short, halting phrases.

Then, it was over. No, Ben didn't want to go to a meeting. No, he wouldn't take another copy of our Big Book.

"We'll come back tomorrow," John said.

Ben nodded and turned back to his drink. He took a long pull as we left.

When John and I returned to the motel the next morning, there was no an-swer to our knock on the door. We went to the motel office.

"He beat it early this morning," the clerk said. "Left at first light and didn't pay the bill. He knew we were going to throw him out today. The last I saw of him, he was walking down the side of the highway with his backpack."

The clerk's description burned a picture into my mind, and it's been there ever since. I don't know if Ben ever got sober. He may still be suffering, or in jail, or dead. Except for that brief moment of connection, I couldn't do anything for him.

It's been many years since that happened, but for as long as I live and work this program, I will remember Ben and my first Twelfth Step call. I may not have done much for him, but he launched me on a journey of countless answers to the call, including some that have been the most meaningful experiences of my life. Some of the people I visited got sober; most did not.

Often I see them in my mind's eye, walking down life's highway, carrying their whole world in a backpack. I thank them for their sacrifice and for what they've shown me. Over and over again, I thank them.

Don G.
Temple, Texas

Tattoo

August 2007

I was sitting in a meeting last week and I heard a newcomer say, with shame in his voice, that he has tattoos on eighty-five percent of his body. Now sober, he regrets them. I certainly identified. I remembered coming to after a long night of drinking. I had an ugly, large tattoo of a spider hanging from its web in my groin area. I have no idea where it came from, who gave it to me, or other details of the night.

When I came into the halls of AA, I was broken—mentally, physically and spiritually. I, too, was full of shame and it was a barrier to connecting with oth-ers. I was a teenage runaway at thirteen, and I survived hand-to-mouth for many years, doing whatever it took to survive on the streets. It was a time of hard drinking and drugging. I loved no one and no one loved me. Every day that I was alive was an unanswered death wish. God and religion were some of the reasons I left home. I had parents who preached virtue while they tortured the children.

There was no God to save me, although I prayed every night with a rosary pressed into my hand.

My tattoos were badges of honor with the hooligans I hung out with. Whenever we survived a particular event, like a thievery or a street trauma, we were honored with a tattoo. They aren't the pretty little things women have today, but the old jailhouse-ink type, where the needle is wrapped in thread and everything from India ink to mascara is used. I have tattoos up both legs, from ankle to thigh, and several on my arms and back.

It was a long road to happy, joyous and free. Because of my visible past, my shame was overwhelming. Women in the halls didn't approach me—I was in-your-face unapproachable. I thought I was having a brilliant rebellion, and these people had no idea where a low-bottom woman drunk could go. If they did, there was judgment (without mercy) that went with that knowledge. But most of that judgment came from myself. I compared stories and didn't identify. Apparently, women had not been to the places I had been and then come into the halls. I was unique.

I kept going to meetings, even when I didn't understand why. I just knew that I didn't want to drink, and the people in the halls said they weren't drinking.

The first time I heard Joe talk about being homeless and in psych wards, I began to identify. It was my first moment of grace. I was not unique. I began to listen to the men, since they were comrades from the streets. Although I didn't get a formal sponsor, I managed to get some advisors around me. Of course, they were male, but they shared the same kind of experiences that I'd had, and I was sure that I didn't cross any personal boundaries.

Today, I am fifty years old and twelve years sober. My tattoos are still a constant reminder of where I came from, and they bring me honor in a different way: They are the reason why some people immediately feel comfortable around me. They know that I didn't learn all that I know in a book.

I went to college and graduated cum laude with a bachelor's degree in psychology. I share the message and do Twelfth Step work with homeless people and sex workers who are alcoholic and addicted. When I come back in from the streets, after sharing my experience, strength and hope, I say, "There, but for the grace of God, go I."

Today, I love my life and myself. I have thrown myself into the middle of the herd with service work. I know and respect many people in recovery. I sponsor women from the street, and I often tell my story to help lift the shame from others. I found a God of my understanding in my Native American grandmother's story of the Butterfly Nation. I got my last tattoo professionally done. It's a butterfly, of course.

Cindy C.
Manchester, New Hampshire

THE TWELVE STEPS

1. We admitted we were powerless over alcohol—that our lives had become unmanageable.
2. Came to believe that a Power greater than ourselves could restore us to sanity.
3. Made a decision to turn our will and our lives over to the care of God as we understood Him.
4. Made a searching and fearless moral inventory of ourselves.
5. Admitted to God, to ourselves, and to another human being the exact nature of our wrongs.
6. Were entirely ready to have God remove all these defects of character.
7. Humbly asked Him to remove our shortcomings.
8. Made a list of all persons we had harmed, and became willing to make amends to them all.
9. Made direct amends to such people wherever possible, except when to do so would injure them or others.
10. Continued to take personal inventory and when we were wrong promptly admitted it.
11. Sought through prayer and meditation to improve our conscious contact with God as we understood Him, praying only for knowledge of His will for us and the power to carry that out.
12. Having had a spiritual awakening as the result of these steps, we tried to carry this message to alcoholics, and to practice these principles in all our affairs.

THE TWELVE TRADITIONS

1. Our common welfare should come first; personal recovery depends upon A.A. unity.

2. For our group purpose there is but one ultimate authority—a loving God as He may express Himself in our group conscience. Our leaders are but trusted servants; they do not govern.

3. The only requirement for A.A. membership is a desire to stop drinking.

4. Each group should be autonomous except in matters affecting other groups or A.A. as a whole.

5. Each group has but one primary purpose—to carry its message to the alcoholic who still suffers.

6. An A.A. group ought never endorse, finance or lend the A.A. name to any related facility or outside enterprise, lest problems of money, property and prestige divert us from our primary purpose.

7. Every A.A. group ought to be fully self-supporting, declining outside contributions.

8. Alcoholics Anonymous should remain forever nonprofessional, but our service centers may employ special workers.

9. A.A., as such, ought never be organized; but we may create service boards or committees directly responsible to those they serve.

10. Alcoholics Anonymous has no opinion on outside issues; hence the A.A. name ought never be drawn into public controversy.

11. Our public relations policy is based on attraction rather than promotion; we need always maintain personal anonymity at the level of press, radio, and films.

12. Anonymity is the spiritual foundation of all our traditions, ever reminding us to place principles before personalities.

Alcoholics Anonymous

AA's program of recovery is fully set forth in its basic text, *Alcoholics Anonymous* (commonly known as the Big Book), now in its Fourth Edition, as well as in *Twelve Steps and Twelve Traditions*, *Living Sober*, and other books. Information on AA can also be found on AA's website at www.aa.org, or by writing to: Alcoholics Anonymous, Box 459, Grand Central Station, New York, NY 10163. For local resources, check your local telephone directory under "Alcoholics Anonymous." Four pamphlets, "This is A.A.," "Is A.A. For You?," "44 Questions," and "A Newcomer Asks" are also available from AA.

AA Grapevine

AA Grapevine is AA's international monthly journal, published continuously since its first issue in June 1944. The AA pamphlet on AA Grapevine describes its scope and purpose this way: "As an integral part of Alcoholics Anonymous for more than sixty years, Grapevine publishes articles that reflect the full diversity of experience and thought found within the AA fellowship. No one viewpoint or philosophy dominates its pages, and in determining content, the editorial staff relies on the principles of the Twelve Traditions." AA Grapevine also publishes La Viña, AA's Spanish-language print magazine, which serves the Hispanic AA community.

In addition to magazines, AA Grapevine, Inc. also produces books, eBooks, audiobooks, and other items. It also offers a Grapevine Online subscription, which includes: five new stories weekly, AudioGrapevine (the audio version of the magazine), Grapevine Story Archive (the entire collection of Grapevine articles), and the current issue of Grapevine and La Viña in HTML format. A Story Archive subscription is also available individually. For more information on AA Grapevine, or to subscribe to any of these, please visit the magazine's website at www.aagrapevine.org or write to:

AA Grapevine, Inc.
475 Riverside Drive
New York, NY 10115